"Think of this book as a great skating instructor. Shyness and social anxiety push us to stay at the edge of the social skating rink, grasping tightly to a safety bar. Vitality and involvement cannot happen there. This book takes you by the hand and teaches you how to maintain your balance and choose your direction while in the open rink of full social participation. Are you fed up with living at the anxious edge of life? Release your grip on the safety bar and grab this book instead—it's time to go for it."

—**Steven C. Hayes, PhD**, foundation professor of psychology at the University of Nevada, Reno and author of *Get Out of Your Mind and Into Your Life*

"This well-written, accessible workbook describes a new approach for coping with social anxiety and shyness based on rigorous research by the authors and others. This book is an excellent resource for anyone who experiences anxiety in social and performance situations. I strongly recommend it!"

—**Martin M. Antony, PhD, ABPP**, professor of psychology at Ryerson University and author of *The Shyness and Social Anxiety Workbook*

"This beautifully written book will benefit anyone suffering from shyness and social anxiety. The authors have a deep understanding and compassion for these difficulties, and their book is full of interesting and helpful exercises, all clearly explained and organized."

—**Ruth Baer, PhD**, professor of psychology at the University of Kentucky, and editor of *Mindfulness-Based Treatment Approaches* and *Assessing Mindfulness and Acceptance Processes in Clients*

"Jan Fleming and Nancy Kocovski have created a highly accessible guide to support the journey from anxiety to calm, from worry to clarity, for those who experience stress in the face of social engagements and new situations. Built upon carefully studied clinical applications and the rigorous science of focusing the mind in an open and peaceful way, this practical handbook offers health-creating relief for anyone with an anxious disposition—especially those with social anxiety and shyness—so that they can find the inner peace and interpersonal confidence needed to live their lives with more ease and well-being. Congratulations to the authors for bringing the research-proven benefits of mindfulness to the lives of so many who are sure to benefit from their empirically-proven and practical suggestions!"

—**Daniel J. Siegel, MD**, executive director at the Mindsight Institute, clinical professor at the David Geffen School of Medicine at UCLA, and author of *Mindsight, The Pocket Guide to Interpersonal Neurobiology*, and *The Mindful Brain*

"This book captures the most cutting-edge approaches for managing one of the most common, chronic, and debilitating psychological problems. Instead of trying to manage or get rid of social anxiety, the authors offer a shift in thinking toward how anxiety is transformed with an open, receptive attitude, and how a person can make progress toward meaningful life pursuits despite the presence of doubt and social fears. Many people will be helped by the insights in this workbook."

—**Todd B. Kashdan, PhD**, associate professor of psychology at George Mason University and author of *Curious? Discover the Missing Ingredient to a Fulfilling Life*

"The authors bring their expertise and caring approach to each of the well-thought-out steps that lead to reducing anxiety over a wide range of situations. The specific therapeutic techniques of acceptance and commitment therapy and mindfulness are translated very skillfully into exercises that lead the reader gradually, step by step, to being able to look at their own anxiety in new ways."

—**Richard P. Swinson, MD, FRCPC**, professor emeritus at Michael G. DeGroote School of Medicine, McMaster University, Hamilton, ON, and author of *The Shyness and Social Anxiety Workbook*

The
Mindfulness & Acceptance Workbook for Social Anxiety & Shyness

Using Acceptance & Commitment Therapy to Free Yourself from Fear & Reclaim Your Life

JAN E. FLEMING, MD
NANCY L. KOCOVSKI, PhD

New Harbinger Publications, Inc.

"Fusion" and "Defusion" illustrations used by permission of Joseph Ciarrochi.

"The Observing Mountain" adapted from the book WHEREVER YOU GO, THERE YOU ARE by Jon Kabat-Zinn, Ph.D. Copyright © 1994 Jon Kabat-Zinn, Ph.D. Used by permission of Hyperion. All rights reserved.

"Body Scan" and "Mindful Stretching" from FULL CATASTROPHE LIVING by Jon Kabat-Zinn, copyright © 1990 by Jon Kabat-Zinn. Used by permission of Dell Publishing, a division of Random House, Inc. Any third party use of this material, outside of this publication, is prohibited. Interested parties must apply directly to Random House, Inc. for permission.

Distributed in Canada by Raincoast Books

Copyright © 2013 by Jan E. Fleming and Nancy L. Kocovski
New Harbinger Publications, Inc.
5674 Shattuck Avenue
Oakland, CA 94609
www.newharbinger.com

Cover design by Amy Shoup; Acquired by Catharine Meyers; Edited by Nelda Street

Library of Congress Cataloging-in-Publication Data

Fleming, Jan E.
 The mindfulness and acceptance workbook for social anxiety and shyness : using acceptance and commitment therapy to free yourself from fear and reclaim your life / Jan E. Fleming, MD and Nancy L. Kocovski, PhD.
    pages cm
 Summary: "Two leading social anxiety researchers present The Mindfulness and Acceptance Workbook for Social Anxiety and Shyness, an acceptance and commitment therapy (ACT)-based workbook filled with assessments and exercises designed to help those with social anxiety or shyness. The book includes a companion CD with guided mindfulness exercises and worksheets"-- Provided by publisher.
 Includes bibliographical references.
 ISBN 978-1-60882-080-1 (pbk.) -- ISBN 978-1-60882-081-8 (pdf e-book) (print) -- ISBN 978-1-60882-082-5 (epub) 1. Social phobia--Treatment. 2. Bashfulness. 3. Acceptance and commitment therapy. I. Kocovski, Nancy L. II. Title.
 RC552.S62F54 2013
 616.85'225--dc23
                        2013009843

Printed in the United States of America

15   14   13

10   9   8   7   6   5   4   3   2   1   First printing

For my husband, Mitch,
for your love, your support, and your faith in me.

—J. E. F.

For my husband, Jim.

—N. L. K.

Contents

PART 1
Fundametals

PART 2
Putting It All Together

Dear Reader,

Welcome to New Harbinger Publications. New Harbinger is dedicated to publishing books based on acceptance and commitment therapy (ACT) and its application to specific areas. New Harbinger has a long-standing reputation as a publisher of quality, well-researched books for general and professional audiences.

As part of New Harbinger's commitment to publishing books based on sound, scientific, clinical research, we oversee all prospective books for the Acceptance and Commitment Therapy Series. Serving as series editors, we comment on proposals and offer guidance as needed, and use a gentle hand in making suggestions regarding the content, depth, and scope of each book.

Books in the Acceptance and Commitment Therapy Series:

- Have an adequate database, appropriate to the strength of the claims being made.

- Are theoretically coherent. They will fit with the ACT model and underlying behavioral principles as they have evolved at the time of writing.

- Orient the reader toward unresolved empirical issues.

- Do not overlap needlessly with existing volumes.

- Avoid jargon and unnecessary entanglement with proprietary methods, leaving ACT work open and available.

- Keep the focus always on what is good for the reader.

- Support the further development of the field.

- Provide information in a way that is of practical use to readers.

These guidelines reflect the values of the broader ACT community. You'll see all of them packed into this book in the most helpful format possible.

Sincerely,

Steven C. Hayes, Ph.D., Georg H. Eifert, Ph.D., John Forsyth, Ph.D., and Robyn Walser, Ph.D.

Foreword

by Zindel Segal, PhD

We seem to be living in an age where public rejection sells. How else can we explain the popularity of reality TV shows where anyone can watch an apprentice being fired at work, young women rejected as future runway models, budding singers told they have no talent, or romantic partners who don't get called back after a first date? Watching these shows, it is easy to conclude that these experiences don't linger after a few tears have been shed and some comforting words from the host have been uttered. In real life, however, social anxiety and rejection are not as easily contained. In fact, the lifetime prevalence rates for the point at which such concerns cross the threshold into a clinical disorder are in the double digits. Furthermore, the pervasive influence of these fears in people's lives leads to further retreat and disengagement from healthy routines and social support. This is where *The Mindfulness and Acceptance Workbook for Social Anxiety and Shyness* comes in. It is written by two expert clinician researchers who have brought a novel lens to bear on these difficulties and, as a result, have found innovative and powerful ways of helping people confront these fears in the service of getting closer to their valued life goals. This workbook is carefully linked to a growing body of empirical data—including the authors' own groundbreaking research—that supports the effectiveness of mindfulness and acceptance approaches to social anxiety and shyness.

This accessible and well-organized workbook starts by describing a central mechanism in social anxiety and shyness that has unintended consequences, namely, the devotion to safety. Seen from the anxious person's perspective, safety behaviors and routines protect him or her from taking unnecessary risks in social situations. What can be difficult to appreciate is that this safety comes at a steep price. The perceived success of a "safety first" strategy locks the person into using it with increasing frequency and scope, inevitably reducing opportunities for fresh learning about the validity of the thinking that drives the fears, or even for taking steps to test whether some social situations are truly dangerous.

Drs. Fleming and Kocovski's use of multiple information channels to reveal this "safety mode," by describing its attentional, emotional, cognitive, and behavioral signs, will quickly cue readers to recognize this mode operating in their own experiences. With this as the foundation, the workbook supports the reader's adoption of novel therapeutic strategies drawn from mindfulness meditation and acceptance and commitment therapy (ACT). Through the use of metaphors, exercises, and worksheets for monitoring new experiences, the reader is gently encouraged to engage in tasks that may seem counterintuitive or threatening at first, but are documented to foster growth and reduce suffering. Readers learn how to approach rather than avoid unpleasant emotions, how to gain distance from their anxious thoughts, and how to let go of control agendas. Ultimately, readers learn how to change their relationship to social anxiety and shyness, rather than only seeing the need to eliminate it.

Both comprehensive in its coverage and sufficiently detailed to answer pragmatic questions about how to follow the authors' program, this workbook captures the state of the art in mindfulness- and ACT-based treatment of social anxiety and shyness. Readers will appreciate its modular chapter format, along with the compendium of client narratives and structured home practices. The latter will be especially helpful in showing how to use the therapeutic principles to deal with the challenges around fear and shyness that come up in daily life. Few workbooks succeed at combining therapeutic innovation and clinical wisdom as well as this one, and as a result, Jan Fleming and Nancy Kocovski's efforts will have a significant impact in our field for years to come.

—Zindel V. Segal, PhD
University of Toronto

Acknowledgments

We are extremely grateful for the work of many pioneers in the areas of mindfulness and acceptance, especially Jon Kabat-Zinn, Zindel Segal, and Steven Hayes. Our own work has been immensely inspired and influenced by their ideas, writings, and teachings. We want to further acknowledge our colleague and mentor Zindel Segal for writing the foreword to this book and (along with Ferris Urbanowski, Susan Woods, and Mark Lau) for training us in mindfulness-based cognitive therapy (MBCT). We are very thankful to Jon Kabat-Zinn for introducing mindfulness to medical and lay communities around the world. We are grateful for the many excellent trainings and workshops we have attended, and for outstanding books we have read by leaders in the acceptance and commitment therapy (ACT) community, especially Steven Hayes, Kelly Wilson, and Russ Harris. We are also appreciative of the ongoing support and wisdom of the broader ACT community.

We want to thank Neil Rector and the Centre for Addiction and Mental Health in Toronto for their support of our pilot work with mindfulness and acceptance–based group therapy (MAGT). We thank the Ontario Mental Health Foundation for its generous support (awarded to Nancy) of our randomized controlled trial (RCT). We owe a big debt of gratitude to Martin Antony and Ryerson University for providing a home for our RCT and supporting it. We want to extend a very heartfelt thank you to all of the study participants and to our individual patients who helped us to refine the approach. Many of Nancy's students were extremely helpful during various stages of our research and the writing of this book, and we thank them for their input.

We are very appreciative of the many helpful comments on earlier drafts of the book provided by Rebecca Blackie, Paul Kelly, Dawn Lloyd, Harriet MacMillan, Jim Naumovski, and Mitch Winnik. We thank John Forsyth and the other New Harbinger ACT series editors for their helpful feedback on our original book proposal. We have valued greatly the assistance and patience of all of those at New Harbinger Publications who contributed to the book, especially Catharine Meyers, Heather Garnos, and Nelda Street. We thank Joseph Ciarrochi for kindly granting us permission to include the two illustrations in chapter 6.

Finally, we want to acknowledge our good friendship and collaboration of eight years; it has been a true pleasure to work together toward helping, in some small way, to make a difference in the lives of individuals who struggle with social anxiety and shyness.

—Jan E. Fleming, MD, FRCPC
University of Toronto
Toronto, Ontario

—Nancy L. Kocovski, PhD
Wilfrid Laurier University
Waterloo, Ontario

This book could not have been written without the unconditional love and support of my husband, Mitch; my amazing sister, Dawn; and my dear friends Harriet, Tom, Gayle, and Theresa. Much gratitude also goes to other friends and family members who never once considered it a bizarre idea to leave an excellent job in order to spend over two years researching and writing a book, and who waited patiently during that time for me to resume living my value of spending precious time with them. I want to thank Jon Kabat-Zinn and Saki Santorelli for introducing me to mindfulness at their excellent seven-day mindfulness-based stress reduction (MBSR) training at Omega Institute in Rhinebeck, New York, in June 1998. I am also grateful for the wise teachings of Jon Kabat-Zinn, Mark Teasdale, and Christina Feldman at a nine-day retreat at Spirit Rock Meditation Center in Woodacre, California, in December 2009. Thanks go to my yoga-teacher extraordinaire,

Mar Jean Olson, for helping to keep me grounded and flexible over these past thirteen years, especially the past two, when I needed it the most! Thanks also to Bryan Murray for his excellent "Postural Alignment through Stretching and Strengthening" classes, which helped to keep me upright after too many hours of hunching over a keyboard. Much appreciation goes to my friends and colleagues at the Ontario chapter of the Association for Contextual Behavioral Science (ACBS) for their enthusiastic support of my valued goal of writing this book. Last, but certainly not least, a big thank you to my patients, who extended their encouragement and good wishes for my writing, even as they struggled with their own issues; I am humbled by your commitment to truly live your values.

—Jan

During the writing of this book, I gave birth to twin boys, Alex and Andrew. Along with their two-year-old sister, Abby, they have inspired me to more strongly focus on what matters. I would like to thank my husband, Jim, for all of his support. Even with three kids under the age of three, my husband has been as strongly supportive of my career as ever. I would like to thank my parents, Risto and Luba, and my brother, Bobby, for all of their help and support. In particular, I am extremely grateful for all of the time they happily spent with their grandchildren, niece, and nephews so that I could focus on this book.

—Nancy

Introduction

If you have picked up this book, chances are that you are one of the approximately 20 percent of adults who experience significant fear of public speaking, or one of the 15 percent (or so) who are very anxious about meeting new people (Ruscio et al. 2008). You are not alone! If you are reading this book, it is also likely that you are not living the life you truly want, that struggling with social fear has kept you from getting the most out of your friendships, family relationships, work, and play. How did this happen, and what can you do about it?

A New Perspective on Social Anxiety and Shyness

In this book, we walk you through a new perspective for understanding and dealing with your social anxiety and shyness. We show you how the root of your suffering may reside in four things that you do in social situations: pay attention to "social danger," resist anxious feelings, buy into anxious thoughts, and avoid your fears instead of doing what really matters to you. We refer to this as acting in "safety mode," and we present you with an alternative, "vital-action mode." In this new mode of action, you will learn how to be fully present in social situations, and how to let go of your struggle with anxious thoughts and feelings so that you can focus on what is most important to you: your values and goals. We will teach you how to do these things using principles and strategies that are part of a new psychotherapy approach called *acceptance and commitment therapy* (or *ACT*, pronounced as a word, not initials) (Hayes, Strosahl, and Wilson 1999).

The ACT Approach

The goal of ACT is to help you open up to difficult thoughts and feelings while doing what is important to you. ACT teaches you how to do this through the use of metaphors and exercises, and by teaching you mindfulness and behavioral strategies. ACT has been shown to be effective for a wide range of problems, including social anxiety, depression, and chronic pain, among others (Ruiz 2010). Next, we want to say a bit about how we came to write this book.

Our Journey to This Book

We first met in 2004, "on the job" at a hospital-based clinic for anxiety problems. Nancy was just a few years into her career as a psychologist, whereas Jan had been practicing psychiatry for almost twenty years; it seemed an unlikely match! However, we soon discovered that we shared a common passion and goal: to help improve the lives of people who were struggling with social anxiety and shyness. In Jan's case, because of her own struggles with social anxiety, especially around public speaking, she had always felt a special connection to her patients whose lives were often tragically diminished by social fears. Nancy had devoted her clinical and research work to understanding and treating social anxiety ever since she had started graduate school in 1996.

Soon after meeting, we decided to work together by coleading *cognitive behavioral therapy* (CBT) groups for outpatients with social anxiety, an approach backed by ample research (Heimberg 2002). At the same time, we started to hear about the benefits of ACT and other mindfulness and acceptance approaches for a number of anxiety problems, including social anxiety. Intrigued, we embarked on a program of reading about and training in these new approaches. We were soon convinced of their potential benefits for our clients, and decided to develop and assess a new treatment for them: *mindfulness and acceptance–based group therapy* (MAGT) for social anxiety disorder. MAGT is a twelve-week program that is based on ACT and includes mindfulness exercises drawn from *mindfulness-based cognitive therapy*

(MBCT) (Segal, Williams, and Teasdale 2002) and *mindfulness-based stress reduction* (MBSR) (Kabat-Zinn 1990), described further in the boxes. Over a five-year period, we conducted a pilot study of MAGT (Kocovski, Fleming, and Rector 2009) and also compared it to CBT in a randomized controlled trial, the gold-standard approach for testing the effectiveness of a new therapy. Our findings were very promising: MAGT was just as effective as CBT in helping individuals deal with social anxiety disorder in our study (Kocovski et al., under review). As we watched many of our study participants shift from struggling with social anxiety to living more fulfilling lives, we were inspired to make our approach available to a broader audience with this workbook. Fortunately, we are not the only ones hard at work in this area. As we write this introduction, nine studies, carried out in five different countries, have found mindfulness and acceptance–based therapies to be effective for social anxiety disorder (summarized in appendix A). That is very heartening!

Our journey to this book has involved more than our clinical and research work. We have also endeavored to apply mindfulness and acceptance strategies to our own lives, including our struggles. We sincerely hope that you will benefit from these strategies as much as we have.

Mindfulness-based cognitive therapy (MBCT) (Segal, Williams, and Teasdale 2002) is based in part on MBSR and was originally developed to prevent relapse of recurrent major depressive disorder. MBCT has since been adapted for a number of different problems (see, for example, Piet and Hougaard 2011).

Mindfulness-based stress reduction (MBSR) (Kabat-Zinn 1990) was originally developed in 1979 for medical patients dealing with stress. It is an eight-week program in group format that consists of formal mindfulness practices, such as the body scan, mindful yoga, and sitting meditation, as well as informal mindfulness practices. It has been adapted for a wide range of problems, and there are now more than five hundred MBSR clinics around the world (Cullen 2011).

How This Book Is Organized

We have provided you with our approach in a succinct and practical format that will allow you to get started right away on moving toward a more rich and meaningful life. The book is divided into two main parts: part 1, "Fundamentals" (chapters 1 through 6), and part 2, "Putting It All Together" (chapters 7 and 8). Part 1 contains basic definitions and an examination of how acting in "safety mode" may be keeping you from living the life you want. We then proceed to uncovering what really matters in your life and to showing you how mindfulness can help you to stay focused on what is important to you in social situations as you accept anxious feelings and defuse from anxious thoughts. In part 2, we put those skills together into an approach for taking "vital action" in social situations as you gradually step toward your valued goals. Throughout the book are case examples, metaphors, and exercises (many adapted from the materials we used with our groups in the research studies, and some that we have developed more recently) to help you to understand and implement this new approach.

How to Use This Book

Most of the chapters build on each other, so we recommend that you read them in the order in which they appear in the book, completing the relevant exercises as you go along. An alternative is to read through the book without doing any of the exercises, and then go back and do the exercises as you read through the book again. If you would prefer to follow a specific schedule for reading the book and doing the exercises, a "Suggested Eight-Week Schedule" is included at the end of this Introduction.

To help you get the most out of this book, there are guided mindfulness exercises (audio downloads available at www.newharbinger.com/20801; see the back of the book for more information), and you can download many of the written exercises there too. For exercises that can be printed from the website, you will see this mouse icon 🖱 . For mindfulness exercises that you can listen to, you will see this headphones icon 🎧 .

The Journey Ahead

If you follow the approach in this book, social anxiety will gradually loosen its grip on your life. You will be freed up to do more things than you could do before—with your friends and family, at work and at play, your life will be about what really matters to you. However, your journey to a more vital life will take hard work, perseverance, and time; there is no point in rushing through the process. Instead, know that every moment you set aside to work with this book will be not only a step toward a more meaningful life, but also a precious gift to yourself.

Suggested Eight-Week Schedule for the Workbook*

Week	Things to Do
1	**Social-Anxiety Playing Field & Safety Mode** Read, and do the exercises, in chapters 1 & 2.
2	**Values and Goals** Read, and do the exercises, in chapter 3. Note: The Values and Goals Worksheet can be revised if necessary in week 6 (see below).
3	**Getting Started with Mindfulness** Read, and do the exercises, in chapter 4. Practice using an observer image (mountain, with or without audio, and others), 5 to 10 minutes, daily. Mindfulness of routine activities (e.g. eating, seeing, hearing, and so on), 5 to 10 minutes, daily Record all mindfulness activities in the Mindfulness Log.
4	**Acceptance of Bodily Sensations (Abs)** Read, and do the exercises, in chapter 5. Do the Body Scan and Mindful Stretching on alternate days (with or without audio); do one session of Being With Your Anxiety, daily. Use the Abs Recording Form to track your experiences. Continue with the observer image, and mindfulness of routine activities, as in week 3 (above).
5	**Defusing from Anxious Thoughts** Read, and do the exercises, in chapter 6. Practice defusion strategies, daily (Record in the Worksheet: Defusing from your Anxious Thoughts). Continue to do the Body Scan and Mindful Stretching on alternate days, as well as one session of Being With Your Anxiety, daily, as in week 4 (above). Mindfulness of routine activities, 5 to 10 minutes, daily
6	**Pause and Practice** Revise your Values and Goals Worksheet (exercise 3.2) if necessary. Practice defusion strategies, daily. Abs: your choice of Body Scan, Mindful Stretching, or Being with Your Anxiety, daily Mindfulness of routine activities, 5 to 10 minutes, daily
7	**Taking VITAL Action** First half of the week: read, and do the exercises, in chapter 7. Second half of the week: review sections of chapter 7 that require more attention. Imagining VITAL Action exercise, daily (with or without audio) Your choice of other mindfulness practices from earlier weeks, daily
8	**Stepping Toward your Future** Read chapter 8. Revise your Goal-Choosing Worksheet; complete Goal-Stepping Worksheets for your goals. Create a schedule for your first full week of "taking VITAL action". Loving-Kindness exercise, daily (with or without audio) Your choice of other mindfulness practices from earlier weeks, daily

*Refer to the relevant chapters of the workbook for exercises, mindfulness practices, and worksheets; some are available at www.newharbinger.com/20801.

PART 1

Fundamentals

CHAPTER 1

Defining Social Anxiety and Shyness

Emily is a thirty-year-old office worker who has been shy for as long as she can remember. She is nervous around most people, especially strangers, and worries that she has nothing interesting to say and that people find her boring. She spends most of her time engaged in solitary hobbies and keeps to herself at work. Lately, she has been feeling very lonely and has come to the realization that she truly wants to connect more with other people: to have more friends (including a boyfriend) and better relationships with her neighbors and coworkers. Emily has been trying to build up the courage to meet new people by taking classes in art or photography, but the thought of having to introduce herself to a class full of strangers is overwhelming. She worries that other people will hear her shaky voice and think she is weird or a weak person. She would love to join a gym but is concerned that her shaky hands will be so obvious that people will ask her what's wrong, causing her to feel completely singled out and embarrassed. She would rather just blend in and not be noticed for any reason. She has considered joining a dating service but can't imagine that any guy would find her interesting enough to go out with her. Emily is very disappointed with the way her life has turned out so far and isn't sure how to make things better.

Jack was recently promoted to a managerial position, a promotion he accepted with extreme reluctance because of the public-speaking demands of the job. Jack is fairly comfortable socializing with others but has had a very hard time with public speaking, dating back to a disastrous classroom speech in seventh grade. Jack recalls that after the first line of his speech, his mind went blank, his heart was racing, and he felt dizzy. He told the teacher he wasn't feeling well, so she sent him to the nurse. He was sure he could see his classmates making fun of him as he left the room. Since then, Jack has been fearful of getting anxious and messing up again, so he has avoided public speaking at all costs. He declined to be best man at his brother's wedding, let his wife do all the talking at his own wedding, and chose jobs that didn't require much in the way of presentations or participation in meetings.

He had wanted to turn down this promotion, but was too embarrassed to tell his boss about his anxiety. Now, in this new position, Jack will have to chair weekly meetings, and give presentations for upper management and for clients. Whenever he allows himself to think about these new responsibilities, his mind fills with worries: that his mind will go blank, that his heart will race so fast he won't be able to speak, that coworkers will notice that he is anxious and think there's something wrong with him. The worries seem endless. Jack is currently well respected among his colleagues, and he fears that everything will fall apart: they will discover that he is incompetent and incapable of doing his job. Jack cannot see how he is going to cope in this new role.

The stories of Emily and Jack are typical of people who experience shyness and social anxiety, defined next.

Shyness and Social Anxiety

Shyness refers to the tendency to feel nervous or timid when interacting with other people, especially strangers. *Social anxiety* is a broader term that includes shyness, as well as the experience of fear when being observed by others (for example, while eating) and performing in front of others (for example, giving a speech). Interacting with others, being observed by others, and performing in front of others are the main types of feared social situations. Shy and socially anxious people are nervous in these situations because of what might happen, because of feared outcomes; specifically, they fear that they will say or do something embarrassing (such as spill a drink or forget their lines), show symptoms of anxiety (such as blushing, trembling, and sweating), or otherwise be scrutinized and judged critically by others (for example, as clumsy, incompetent, weak, and so on). We saw that Emily's shyness centers on her fears of being judged as boring, weak, or weird. Jack is worried that his anxiety will cause him to mess up during presentations and that it ultimately will lead to his being judged incompetent in his job. The specific details of feared outcomes vary considerably from person to person; however, just as "all roads lead to Rome," most social fears come down to a concern about coming up short in the eyes of others.

The intensity of shyness and social anxiety, and the range of feared social situations also vary a lot from person to person. Some people are just a little shy with strangers, while others are intensely shy with almost everyone they encounter. Some people fear a single type of social situation (such as giving speeches), whereas others are anxious in most types of social situations. When social fears interfere significantly in your life, that may indicate a clinical syndrome called social anxiety disorder.

Social Anxiety Disorder

Social anxiety disorder (SAD), also known as *social phobia*, is a term used by researchers and clinicians. The five main diagnostic criteria for SAD are quoted in the following list from the *Diagnostic and Statistical Manual of Mental Disorders, Fourth Edition, Text Revision* (American Psychiatric Association 2004, 456) (some words about using the diagnosis in children have been omitted).

DSM-IV-TR Diagnostic Criteria for Social Anxiety Disorder

1. A marked and persistent fear of one or more social or performance situations in which the person is exposed to unfamiliar people or to possible scrutiny by others. The individual fears that he or she will act in a way (or show anxiety symptoms) that will be humiliating or embarrassing….

2. Exposure to the feared social situation almost invariably provokes anxiety, which may take the form of a…panic attack [defined in the next section]….

3. The person recognizes that the fear is excessive or unreasonable….

4. The feared social or performance situations are avoided, or else are endured with intense anxiety or distress.

5. The avoidance, anxious anticipation, or distress in the feared social or performance situation(s) interferes significantly with the person's normal routine, occupational (academic) functioning, or social activities or relationships, or there is marked distress about having the phobia.

The second criterion mentions the occurrence of anxiety symptoms, which may reach the intensity of a "panic attack," defined next.

Panic Attack

A *panic attack* is a period of intense anxiety that develops rapidly and includes at least four of the following symptoms, as quoted in the following list from *DSM-IV-TR* (American Psychiatric Association 2004, 432):

- palpitations, pounding heart, or accelerated heart rate

- sweating

- trembling or shaking

- sensations of shortness of breath or smothering

- feeling of choking

- chest pain or discomfort

- nausea or abdominal distress

- feeling dizzy, unsteady, light-headed, or faint

- derealization (feelings of unreality) or depersonalization (being detached from oneself)

- fear of losing control or going crazy

- fear of dying

- paresthesias (numbness or tingling sensations)

- chills or hot flushes

Panic attacks are believed to be part of a biological defense system that developed in humans and other species to respond to types of danger (for example, lions, poisonous snakes, enemy tribe members) that require rapid responses, such as fighting, fleeing, or freezing. This system increases the heart rate (and breathing rate) to get blood and oxygen to the muscles, tenses the muscles for action, induces sweating to cool the body (and make it slippery if your enemy grabs you), and does other things to prepare your body to respond to danger. When some socially anxious people encounter a potential "social danger"—when a feared outcome, such as feeling embarrassed, seems imminent—their bodies respond as if a lion were present, just as Jack's did during his seventh-grade speech. Jan has experienced a number of panic attacks over the years, all of which have been triggered by a request to speak in a group when she has not been prepared. Caught off guard in these situations, her heart starts to pound out of her chest, her mind goes completely blank, and an image of herself pops into her mind—mouth open and speechless, or else uttering gibberish. Other socially anxious people experience fewer and less-intense physical symptoms of anxiety, while others are not bothered by physical symptoms at all.

Regardless of whether you experience one physical symptom of anxiety or ten, fear one type of social situation or many types, or fulfill some or all criteria for a diagnosis of SAD, you will find the strategies discussed in this book to be helpful.

Now that we've defined some terms, let's take a look at the types of social situations that trigger your anxiety.

Situations That Trigger Social Anxiety

As you saw earlier in this chapter, feared social situations can be roughly divided into those involving interaction with others, being observed by others, and performing in front of others. Keep in mind that there is some overlap among the categories, with some social situations fitting into more than one category.

Situations Involving Social Interaction

Situations that involve social interaction, or talking with others, typically occur throughout our day-to-day lives: at work, at school, at home, at social gatherings, and in public places. Chatting with coworkers, placing a coffee order, asking for directions, and mingling at a party are all examples of situations involving social interaction. You may find that your experience of shyness in these types of situations depends on whom you are talking with, your role in the conversation, or a number of other specifics about the situation. One way to get at the specifics of your situations involving social interaction is to combine your responses to the following two questions:

1. When your anxiety is triggered during a conversation, with whom are you speaking? Check (√) all that apply to you:

_____ strangers

_____ neighbors

_____ acquaintances

_____ friends

_____ family members

_____ coworkers

_____ romantic partner, spouse, or date

_____ authority figure (for example, boss, professor, doctor, police officer)

_____ salesperson

_____ one person

_____ group of people

_____ other: _____

2. When your anxiety is triggered, what are you doing in the conversation? Check (√) all that apply to you:

_____ engaging in small talk

_____ beginning a conversation

_____ keeping a conversation going

_____ ending a conversation

_____ sharing information about yourself

_____ expressing an opinion or disagreement

_____ asking for assistance

_____ asking someone to change his or her behavior

_____ asking someone on a date

_____ speaking on the phone

_____ other: _____

The types of situations involving social interaction that trigger anxiety for you will probably involve combinations of your responses to those two questions (for example, engaging in small talk with strangers, neighbors, and coworkers; sharing information about yourself on a date or in a group of people; expressing disagreement with friends or family members; and so on).

Being Observed by Others

There are many social situations that do not feature talking but still have the potential for people to notice or observe you. You may feel as if you were the center of attention in these situations, as if all eyes were on you. Common situations of this type are listed next. Check (√) all of the situations (if any) where your anxiety shows up.

_____ eating, drinking, or writing in front of others

_____ working in front of others

_____ waiting in line

_____ taking public transportation

_____ walking into a crowded room

_____ walking in public (for example, through a shopping mall or down a busy street)

_____ using a crowded elevator

_____ dancing or exercising in front of others

_____ driving (observed by your passengers or people in other vehicles)

_____ serving food or drinks

_____ using a public restroom when others are nearby

_____ other: _____

Performing in Front of Others

Performance situations can range from formal to informal: people may have paid to see you perform or may be evaluating you for a job, or you might simply "have the floor" as you give a toast at a wedding, speak up at a meeting, or tell a story at a dinner party. However, performing is truly in the eye of the beholder; any social situation can feel like a performance. Many of our clients have expressed that even a simple conversation feels like a performance!

In which of these common performance situations (if any) is your anxiety triggered? Check (√) all that apply to you.

_____ public speaking

_____ introducing yourself to a group

_____ speaking up at a meeting

_____ asking a question in a class

_____ singing in front of people

_____ playing a musical instrument

_____ acting

_____ performing a dance

_____ playing a sport

_____ taking a test

_____ being interviewed for a job (or being asked questions for some other reason)

_____ other: _____

Next, considering your responses for all three types of situations, describe your top three feared social situations, the ones that are most problematic for you in your life. First, look at the situations chosen by Emily and Jack.

Sample Exercise 1.1   Top Three Feared Social Situations

Emily

1. *Any kind of small talk, especially with strangers*

2. *Dating, especially sharing stuff about myself*

3. *Introducing myself to a group*

Jack

1. *Speaking up in a meeting at work*

2. *Giving a presentation at work, especially when the boss is there*

3. *Giving speeches at family events (like weddings and funerals)*

Now it's your turn. We'll be asking you to refer to your top three feared social situations for some of the exercises in the following chapters, so it's a good idea to print the following worksheet from the website at www.newharbinger.com/20801 and keep your responses handy.

Exercise 1.1   Top Three Feared Social Situations

Describe the three social situations that are most problematic for you in your life:

1. _____

2. _____

3. _____

If you found it difficult to come up with three situations, that's fine; you may think of other situations as you proceed through the book. It's also fine to change your mind about which situations are your top three; be sure to modify your list if that happens.

In the remaining chapters, as we examine what is going wrong in your feared social situations (and how to address the problem), we will be using the metaphor of a playing field, where your feared social situations (your top three and others) are your *social-anxiety playing field*. Now, on playing fields that are used for sports (such as baseball and soccer), you can see people engaged in different *modes of action*, each with its own goal: in "practice mode" the goal might be to improve skills and strategies for an upcoming game, in "competition mode" the goal is to beat your opponent, and in "fun mode" the goal is to enjoy yourself and have a good time. In a similar way, on your social-anxiety playing field, you can be engaged in different modes of action with different goals.

In the next chapter, we introduce you to "safety mode," a mode of action that is very likely contributing to problems for you on your social-anxiety playing field and in your life.

CHAPTER 2

Safety Mode: The Costs of Pursuing "Safety"

In a scientific paper titled "Shyness and Boldness in Humans and Other Animals," the prominent evolutionist David Sloan Wilson and his colleagues (1994) tell a sweet story about a shy sunfish, a little guy that preferred to dine in the company of his more outgoing, bold friend. One day, researchers removed his bold buddy from the pond. His response was to hide under a submerged tree stump for *three days*, refusing to come out to eat until his friend was returned! Can you relate to that story? Perhaps you have stayed close to a "safe" friend at a party, only to end up hiding in the restroom when your friend wandered off. If so, you were operating in *safety mode*, the subject of this chapter.

Safety Mode

Safety mode is about staying out of harm's way, about pursuing "safety." Your goal in safety mode is to protect yourself from your feared outcomes. Those outcomes, also known as *social danger*, include embarrassing yourself, showing anxiety symptoms, and coming up short in the eyes of others (as outlined in the previous chapter). There are four main components of safety mode, four things that happen as you struggle to keep safe: you use safety behaviors, you focus on social danger, you resist your anxious feelings, and you *fuse with* your anxious thoughts. Next, we will describe the individual components of safety mode, starting with safety behaviors.

Safety Behaviors

Safety behaviors, such as sticking with a "safe" friend at a party, are the things you do to protect yourself from social danger. In this section, we will help you to identify your safety behaviors and examine the costs of using them on your social-anxiety playing field, the costs of pursuing safety. Safety behaviors can be roughly divided into *outright avoidance* and *other safety behaviors*, both of which are discussed next.

Outright Avoidance

Outright avoidance involves staying away from your feared social situations, just as Jack avoided all types of public speaking and Emily avoided most opportunities to socialize. Outright avoidance can appear, at first glance, to be a foolproof way to keep you out of harm's way: if you don't give the speech, you can't mess it up; if you don't ask him out, he can't turn you down; if you stay away from the party, they can't see how nervous you are; and so on. However, this approach to avoiding social danger can put you in the way of a different, more insidious type of danger: the danger of a life not lived. With each invitation you turn down, each meeting you skip, and each conversation you avoid, your life becomes a little more restricted. In the worst-case scenario, your life can become so small that it hardly seems worth living.

Outright avoidance can also backfire and lead to the very outcome you fear, as seen in the poem *Fear*, by the popular children's author, Shel Silverstein (2009). The poem is about a boy who is so afraid of drowning that he spends all of his time trying to avoid water. He becomes so unhappy with his life of avoidance that he cries and cries, and ends up drowning in his tears! Has avoiding social situations ever backfired on you? It happened to Ben, one of our group members who had an intense fear of disappointing people. During his first year of college, he fell into a pattern of canceling plans with his friends at the last minute, out of concern that his shyness would put a damper on things. His friends saw this as snubbing them, and they actually *were* disappointed in him as a result—the very thing he had been trying to avoid!

What have been the costs of outright avoidance in *your* life? In the following exercise, list the social situations (if any) that you currently avoid or have avoided, along with any costs associated with that avoidance. First look at how Emily and Jack responded.

Sample Exercise 2.1   The Costs of Outright Avoidance

Situations Avoided	Costs of Avoidance
Emily • Going to the gym (for the most part) • Pursuing interesting hobbies • Talking to my coworkers	• I feel lonely and bored most of the time. I hate my life.
Jack: • *Being best man for my brother, Paul* • *Giving a speech at my wedding* • *Jobs that require public speaking*	• *I missed an opportunity to show Paul and all of our family and friends how important he is to me.* • *I still regret not having extended a public thank-you to all of our wonderful guests.* • *The jobs I've ended up in are not best suited to my skills, knowledge, and interests; I have so much more to contribute.*

Now, it's your turn.

Exercise 2.1   The Costs of Outright Avoidance

Situations Avoided	Costs of Avoidance

In addition to outright avoidance, there are many other types of safety behaviors.

Other Safety Behaviors

Other safety behaviors come into play once you are actually "on" your social-anxiety playing field (that is, in your feared social situations). They are geared to minimize your chances of being scrutinized and judged by hiding your anxiety symptoms, keeping you as inconspicuous as possible, and attempting to control the impression you are making. You may use a wide range of safety behaviors, depending on the specifics of your fears and of the social situations you encounter. Here is a list (by no means exhaustive) of some typical safety behaviors that are used by socially anxious people:

- *To hide anxiety:* Wear makeup or clothing to hide blushing, wear clothing to hide or minimize sweating, hold a glass tightly to hide shaky hands, or hide emotions by keeping a neutral face.

- At *social gatherings:* Go with a "safe" friend, talk to "safe" people, or help out in the kitchen (or engage in other helping activities to avoid conversations).

- *During conversations:* Keep attention off yourself by asking lots of questions of others, say as little as possible, speak quickly, carefully plan topics ahead of time, avoid "awkward" pauses, or act "as if" you were someone else.

- *To minimize chances of people getting upset with you:* Always agree, be pleasant, nod and smile, or conceal your opinions.

- *To minimize drawing attention to yourself:* Arrive early to meetings and classes, position yourself so as not to be noticed, or carefully choose a seat.

- *Concerning speeches:* Read it word for word, speak quickly, keep it short, hide behind a lectern, don't leave time for questions, or ask somebody else to do it for you.

- *In public:* Listen to your MP3 player, check your smartphone, read a book, or keep your eyes down.

- *At restaurants:* Choose food that isn't messy, order what others have ordered to avoid choosing the "wrong" thing, or don't send back food or otherwise complain about the food or service.

- *Concerning drinking:* Have a few drinks at social events to "calm your nerves," or don't drink (to avoid embarrassing yourself).

The costs of using these types of safety behaviors are typically not as dramatic as for outright avoidance. After all, at least you made it into the situations; however, they can be costly in a number of different ways. Specifically, for all of the time and effort that goes into pursuing safety, there is less opportunity to do other things that are important to you: perhaps getting to know people, trying out new foods, and contributing your opinions, to name a few. As you restrict your actions and attempt to "blend in," you can miss out on fully experiencing the richness that many social situations have to offer, miss out on fully participating in your life. Also, if some social situations go okay when you are using safety behaviors, you may come to believe that your safety behaviors are required in order for you to "survive" social situations. So you continue to use them and continue to miss out.

In the following exercise, we'll look at some of the safety behaviors you use for protection in your top three feared social situations from chapter 1, along with any costs of those behaviors. First, look at how Emily and Jack responded.

Emily's Exercise 2.2   What Are You Giving Up for Safety?

List one or more of your safety behaviors (if any) for each of your top three feared social situations, along with any costs of using the behaviors.

Situation 1: *Small talk—I focus on trying to steady my shaky voice; sometimes I try so hard that I lose track of conversations. I also speak really softly to hide my shaky voice; people seem annoyed and are forever asking me to speak up.*

Situation 2: *Dating—I rarely go on dates, but when I do, I keep up a steady stream of questions to my date. I've been told that I'm hard to get to know, and I think I've missed out on a few second dates because of it.*

Situation 3: *Introducing myself to a group—I memorize a very short blurb about myself and volunteer to go first to get it out of the way (and I talk really fast); group members never get to know the "real" me.*

Jack's Exercise 2.2   What Are You Giving Up
for Safety?

List one or more of your safety behaviors (if any) for each of your top three feared social situations, along with any costs of using the behaviors.

Situation 1: *Speaking up at work meetings; I get by with saying as little as possible. As a result, my team misses out on my expertise and I feel like I'm letting them down.*

Situation 2: *Presentations at work; I spend weeks preparing for (and perfecting) even short presentations. It takes precious time away from my family.*

Situation 3: *Speeches at family events; I try to avoid them, but if it isn't possible, I keep them ultra short. I'm not setting a very good example for my nieces and nephews.*

Now, it's your turn.

Exercise 2.2 What Are You Giving Up for Safety?

List one or more of your safety behaviors (if any) for each of your top three feared social situations, along with any costs of using the behaviors.

Situation 1: _____

_____

_____

_____

Situation 2: _____

_____

_____

_____

Situation 3: _____

_____

_____

_____

Taken together, your responses to the previous two exercises may reflect a costly toll: the toll that pursuing safety is taking on your life.

Next, we move on to explore the remaining three components of safety mode: paying attention to social danger, resisting anxious feelings, and fusing with anxious thoughts. We will describe them individually, and show you how they interact as a "team" and feed into your safety behaviors. As we introduce you to the first team member, imagine that you are entering one of your top three feared social situations.

Paying Attention to Social Danger

As you picture yourself in your feared situation, what aspects of yourself are you paying attention to? It is likely that you are paying particular notice to signs that social danger may be lurking in the situation, that you are at risk of embarrassing yourself or making a bad impression. Your attention may be drawn to visible signs of your anxiety (for example, blushing, sweating, trembling), to what you're saying (for example, something boring), or to what you're doing (for example, moving awkwardly, spilling a drink). Now, if you *are* focused on some aspect or aspects of yourself (as you continue to imagine your feared situation), is your anxiety getting weaker or stronger? Most of our clients report that the more they focus on themselves, the more their anxious feelings intensify.

As you continue to imagine your feared situation, you may also notice that you are on "high alert" for other signs of social danger, for signs that people are scrutinizing you or disapproving of you. For example, your focus may be drawn to the person who seems to be staring at you as you walk down the street; your attention may be hijacked by the yawns of audience members as you give your speech; or you may be quick to notice your neighbor frowning as you chat with her. Now, imagine that you *do* notice a frown (or other sign of potential danger in another person). Are you getting more anxious, looking away, or making a plan of escape? For the most part, focusing on social danger (in yourself and others) will tend to intensify your anxiety and feed into safety behaviors.

Resisting Anxious Feelings

Now, let's examine how you are relating to your anxious feelings in your imagined social situation. By anxious feelings we mean the feeling (emotion) of fear and the physical sensations that go along with it, such as palpitations and muscle tension. Although we are focusing on anxious feelings, you may also notice other emotions such as anger and sadness. Are you okay with your anxious feelings, or are you resisting them? Are you willing to fully experience your racing heart or other bodily sensations, or are you pushing them away, trying to control them? In all likelihood, like most people who are shy and socially anxious, you are struggling with your anxious and other feelings. And your mind isn't helping matters, as you will see next.

Fusing with Anxious Thoughts

As you continue to imagine your feared situation, notice what your mind is doing. Is it jumping in with commentary (such as *You're sweating too much, You're going to mess up, He thinks you're stupid*) and suggestions (such as *Don't say anything, Keep smiling, Cover your face*). How are you relating to your anxious thoughts? Are you *fused* with them? In other words, are you getting caught up in your thoughts, buying into them, and doing what they tell you to do? Fusing with anxious thoughts is a very common activity of the socially anxious mind (much more on this in chapter 6).

Now, let's look a bit more at how your "team members" interact and feed into your safety behaviors, using examples from Emily and Jack. (Members of the "team" are indicated in brackets, as well as the costs of keeping safe.)

"Team" Interaction

Emily's attention zooms in on her shaky voice the moment she utters a word during conversations [paying attention to social danger]; she realizes it's "just nerves" but doesn't find this acceptable [resisting anxious feelings]; her mind jumps in (*You sound nervous; they think you're weird*), and she buys into what it's telling her [fusing with anxious thoughts]; she tries to steady her voice and hide it by speaking softly and slowly [using safety behaviors]; at times, she gets so wrapped up in struggling with her shaky voice that she loses track of conversations and feels even more embarrassed [costs of keeping safe].

Jack's attention is captured by his loudly thumping heart whenever he considers speaking up in meetings [paying attention to social danger]; the more he focuses on his heart, the faster it beats; he is not open to feeling this way [resisting anxious feelings]; his mind soon chimes in (*You're going to pass out and look like a fool; better to not say anything*); he buys into what it's saying [fusing with anxious thoughts] and chooses to stay quiet [using safety behaviors]; he always regrets not contributing to the discussion [cost of keeping safe].

On the few occasions that Jack has been brave enough to give a presentation at work, he always seems to notice the yawns of his coworkers whenever he glances up from his notes [paying attention to social danger]. His judging mind is right there to interpret (*You're boring them*) and tell him what to do (*Keep your eyes on your notes; talk faster*); he takes these words very seriously [fusing with anxious thoughts] and hurries to finish his presentation [using safety behaviors]. Sometimes he talks so fast that he leaves out important points [cost of keeping safe]. Recently, a coworker pointed out to Jack that he had been so focused on reading his notes [using safety behaviors] that he had missed a "thumbs up" and nod of encouragement from the boss [cost of keeping safe].

From Emily's and Jack's examples, you can see how focusing on danger, struggling with anxious feelings, and fusing with anxious thoughts all work together to feed your safety behaviors. Given the costs of keeping safe, this is not a team you want "helping" you!

If you felt somewhat disheartened by reading about safety mode, we are pleased to end this chapter with some good news, that there is a better, alternative mode of action on your social-anxiety playing field: *vital-action mode*.

Vital-Action Mode

In contrast to safety mode, the goal in vital-action mode is to live a life that really matters to you. In the remaining chapters, we will teach you the skills necessary for shifting from safety mode to vital-action mode. We will help you get in touch with your values and goals, stay tuned to the present moment, bring acceptance and compassion to difficult feelings, and gain distance from your worries, along with other strategies. With your new skills in hand, you will be ready to start taking steps, at your own pace, toward a new, more vital life.

Now, if you have been operating in safety mode much of the time, you may have lost touch with what you really want in your life. The next chapter will help you with that. It is about "knowing what matters," uncovering your values and goals.

CHAPTER 3

Knowing What Matters: Uncovering Your Values and Goals

Imagine that when you wake up tomorrow, your social anxiety is gone. Take a few moments now to write about how your life would change. What would you do differently in your life? For now, consider how your life would change in terms of your relationships, work or school, and "play"; would you have more friends, a better job, go dancing every weekend? Just go with your gut and write down the first things that come to mind.

If my social anxiety magically disappeared overnight, I would...

_____

_____

_____

_____

That brief exercise was meant to be a sneak peek at what really matters in your life, the subject of this chapter. We are starting here so that you can see, up front, what you are working toward. Just as having a vision of a satisfying career helps to sustain some people through long periods of study or training, we hope that your vision of a life that truly matters to you will help to motivate and inspire you through the difficult work ahead in this book. You'll have a chance to elaborate on that vision after we define values and goals.

Defining Values and Goals

Our favorite way of describing values and goals is with the compass metaphor (Hayes 2005), where values are like the directions of a compass (east, west, north, and south) that guide you on a journey, and goals are like the destinations, the cities and countries you encounter along the way. A value cannot be "arrived at" or "achieved" in the sense of saying it's done, just as the direction of "east" can never be achieved; you can continue to travel east from any destination. For example, let's say that in the area of work, it really matters to you to be a responsible employee. "Being responsible" is a value that will guide your actions and be reflected in "achievable" goals, such as getting to work on time and completing assignments to the best of your ability. You will never be finished with "being responsible"; it will continue to direct and guide your behavior in the job or jobs you hold. In the same vein, the value of "being a good parent" would guide you in your goals of attending parent-teacher meetings and coaching your daughter's hockey team. In sum, values are your life directions, and goals are your life destinations.

Another way to look at values and goals is to notice that they are different aspects of behavior: values are reflected in the ongoing *qualities* of your actions (such as being responsible or being creative), whereas goals are reflected in the concrete *outcomes* of your actions (for example, getting to work on time or writing a poem). Because of this interconnection between values and goals, we often combine the words in phrases such as "values-based goals" or "valued goals." As well, "commitment," the middle term in Acceptance and Commitment Therapy, represents the actions you take toward your valued goals.

As we move further through the territory of identifying your values and goals, we'll be assisted by the stories of John and Camille.

With his wife, Dana, and their two children, John recently moved into a home in their "dream neighborhood," with excellent schools, lots of other young families, and a reputation for being a safe, "closely knit" community. John mostly works from home, which affords him greater flexibility than Dana, who often works long hours at an office. Dana would like for John to share some of the responsibility for the kids' after-school activities: taking their daughter to soccer practice, cheering their son on at hockey games, enrolling the kids in swimming lessons, and carpooling with other parents, to name a few. John is convinced however, that he won't be able to manage small talk with other parents and that he will never be accepted as "one of the gang." He worries that he'll be pegged as boring and inept, "the one to avoid talking to at any cost." So, he has done little to help Dana with the kids, resulting in some tension in their marriage. He even avoids taking care of his lawn and flowers, in case his neighbors are outside at the same time, and is embarrassed at how shabby they look as a result. He watches enviously as other parents and neighbors mingle and chat with apparent ease. John feels that he is letting down his kids, his wife, his community, and himself.

Camille is passionate about protecting the environment, hiking, and bird-watching. She dreams of working at a nonprofit organization, finding a partner with interests similar to hers, and being part of a small group of like-minded friends. Camille hasn't made much progress on the "job front" because of her intense fear of sweating in job interviews; she worries that when potential bosses shake her slippery hand, they will assume she is incompetent. Despite having completed a degree in environmental sciences five years ago, she works as a data-entry clerk at her uncle's firm (no interview was required). She is also wary of meeting new people (handshakes seem to be customary) and has avoided dating, joining local hiking and bird-watching groups, and doing volunteer work as a result. She feels stuck from being in a boring job and having little to do in her free time.

John and Camille both agreed that avoiding their social fears was keeping them from doing what really mattered to them. We asked them to complete the following exercise as a way to get in closer touch with what they wanted to stand for and accomplish in their lives. First, read their responses and then do the exercise yourself.

Sample Exercise 3.1 Attending Your Eightieth Birthday Party

Imagine that you are attending your eightieth birthday party. You have managed to live your life in a way that really matters to you. How would you want your life characterized? What would you want your friends and family to say about you in a speech? First, look at how John and Camille completed this exercise.

John:

John is a great family man. As a father, he always put the needs of his children first, guiding them from infancy to adulthood with love, patience, and respect, and was deeply involved in helping them to become the wonderful parents they both are today. As a grandparent to three gorgeous grandkids, he is beloved as "chauffeur and cheerleader" for many of their practices and games, no matter how early in the morning he has to get himself out the door. As a devoted husband to Dana for fifty-five years, he fully supported her career and shared with her in all of the joy and heartache life presented to them. As well as a great family man, John is also a respected member of his community, someone we can always count on for help, advice, and a friendly chat. We love you, John.

Camille:

I'm sure the first thing that comes to mind for most of us when we think of Camille is her dedication to the environment. Through her amazing career at Greenpeace and tireless volunteer work, she has helped to make our world a safer and cleaner place for all living beings. As well, she and her "partner in crime," Steve, have fearlessly guided us on hiking and birding trips on five continents, allowing us all to experience and appreciate the vast beauty of our precious earth. Camille has already planned our next trip, to Antarctica. So gang, get out your parkas and sign up to see the penguins with our dear friend, Camille!

Now it's your turn.

Exercise 3.1   Attending Your Eightieth
                                          Birthday Party

Imagine that you are attending your eightieth birthday party. You have managed to live your life in a way that really matters to you. How would you want your life characterized? What would you want your friends and family to say about you in a speech?

_____

_____

_____

_____

_____

_____

_____

_____

_____

_____

_____

In doing the exercise, John saw that family-related values are most important to him. Camille had fun with her speech, even if it was a bit "over the top." She was somewhat surprised to see that travel and adventure featured so prominently. What did you discover about your values and goals by doing the exercise?

Another exercise that can be helpful for uncovering values is called "Flip Your Fear," based on the premise that "we feel the most vulnerable in areas that matter to us" (Wilson and Dufrene 2010, 116). So, it's possible to uncover what matters to you by closely examining your vulnerabilities: your fears. For example, behind a fear of "saying the wrong thing," can you see the value of "connecting with others"? In the same vein, can you "flip the fear" of being rejected by others and find the value of "belonging," whether to a family, a group of colleagues, or another group? Can you see that worry about flubbing a speech goes hand in hand with the value of "doing your best"? Try the "Flip Your Fear" exercise yourself. Look closely at your fears, worries, and vulnerabilities, and see if you can "turn them over" to uncover what really matters to you.

My fear is:	The underlying value is:

A couple of other ways to get at your values are as follows:

- Imagine that you have been in a car accident, it's a week later, and you have just awoken from a coma and will fully recover. You vow that you are going to do things differently in life to make the most out of this second chance you have been given. What would you do differently?

- Imagine that you could go back in time to when you were a child, some time prior to when you really started feeling socially anxious. What hopes, dreams, and aspirations can you now see for yourself?

Now that you have some ideas about what really matters in your life, let's delve more deeply into your specific values and goals.

Identifying Your Values and Goals

We are going to explore your values and goals in ten different domains or areas of life (Hayes, Strosahl, and Wilson 1999). As you read the descriptions of each of the following life areas, we will ask you to respond to two questions. The first question, "Is this area important to you?" is asking if you care enough about an area to devote time and effort to it. The second question, "Does this area involve at least one of your feared social situations?" is getting at the relevance of the area to your social anxiety. In this book, we will focus on identifying your values and goals in life domains that are both important to you *and* relevant to your struggle with social anxiety. In choosing your values and goals, please keep these additional points in mind:

- Not everyone places the same importance on individual life areas. Also, not everyone has the same values and goals. This exercise is not about choosing the "right" life areas, or coming up with values and goals that are socially acceptable or politically correct. It's about identifying what you truly value and want in your life. No one else has to read what you have written.

- You may be tempted to include emotions (feelings) in your values (for example, "Try not to be nervous at parties") and goals (for example, "Be calm when you give the speech"). However, this book is not about controlling your emotions and having them "be" a certain way; it is about accepting your feelings and allowing them to be as they are (more on acceptance in chapter 4) so that you can shift from pursuing safety to pursuing what truly matters to you. Instead of "Try not to be nervous at parties," see if something like "Connect with others at parties" would fit for you. Instead of "Be calm when you give the speech," how about "Give the speech (regardless of how you feel) because it's important to you"?

- Some of the life areas overlap. For example, doing yoga could fit under health, spirituality, leisure, or even friendships. It's not important which categories you choose for recording your values and goals, as long as you record them somewhere!

- It's okay if your goals are fairly general at this point (for example, "make new friends"). In chapter 7 we will assist you in breaking your goals into more specific steps (for example, "Introduce myself to Joan at the school picnic").

Let's move now to the individual life areas. We suggest that as you go along, you record your values and goals on the blank "Values and Goals Worksheet" (which you can print from the website at www.newharbinger.com/20801). You can also look at how John and Camille completed their worksheets (see "Sample Exercise 3.2," later in this chapter).

Intimate Relationships

This life area is about your relationship with your "significant other": your current spouse or partner, or the intimate relationship you want to find for yourself if you are not currently in one. To identify your values for this area, think about the type of person you want to be in an intimate relationship. What would be (or are) the ongoing qualities of your actions? Do you value being loving, dependable, or fun, or do you have some other value? To identify your goals for this area, consider the "destinations" of your actions, outcomes that you can check off a list. Perhaps you want to get married, help with chores, go on date nights, say something nice to your partner every day, and so on.

Circle yes or no for the following two questions:

yes   or   no   Is this area important to you?

yes   or   no   Does this area involve at least one of your feared social situations?

If you responded yes to both questions, please identify your values and goals for this life area.

Friendships and Other Social Relationships

This domain involves your relationships with friends, acquaintances, and other people you interact with. To get at your values for this area, ask yourself, *What qualities do I want to bring to friendships and other social relationships?* Some examples include authenticity, openness, assertiveness, dependability, and friendliness. To get at your goals for this domain, consider the number of friends you want, how often you want to see them, and the types of activities you want to engage in together. Other goals for social relationships might include smiling and making eye contact with the people you interact with, or chatting with strangers.

Circle yes or no for the following two questions:

yes   or   no   Is this area important to you?

yes   or   no   Does this area involve at least one of your feared social situations?

If you responded yes to both questions, please identify your values and goals for this life area.

Family Relationships

The family relationships category is about your relationships with your parents, siblings, children, and other family members. In choosing your values and goals for this area, reflect on the kind of family member (child, sibling, parent, and so on) that you really want to be and how that would manifest in your actions. For example, are you as involved with your family as you would like to be? Perhaps you are too involved, like our client Marjorie, who was spending most of her free time helping out her parents and driving her nieces and nephews to various activities. Although helping her family was certainly important to Marjorie, she came to realize that much of her "helping" behavior was actually in the service of avoiding her most feared outcome: the possibility of rejection if she were to open herself up to people outside of her family. In her work with us, she was able to uncover the "hidden" value of independence from her family.

Circle yes or no for the following two questions:

yes   or   no   Is this area important to you?

yes   or   no   Does this area involve at least one of your feared social situations?

If you responded yes to both questions, please identify your values and goals for this life area.

Career/Employment

Are you currently employed? If not, what type of career or job do you want for yourself? What kind of an employee (or employer) do you want to be? Do you value being creative or reliable? Is it important for you to be a good team member or mentor? What other qualities would ideally guide your actions at work? What are some of your work-related goals: getting a job, finding a new career, asking for a raise, providing constructive criticism to an employee, or some other goal?

Circle yes or no for the following two questions:

yes   or   no   Is this area important to you?

yes   or   no   Does this area involve at least one of your feared social situations?

If you responded yes to both questions, please identify your values and goals for this life area.

Education/Learning

In addition to formal education, this domain covers all types of learning and personal growth. What is important to you as a student and learner? Do you value curiosity, diligence, or taking on new challenges? What are your learning goals? They might include finishing a degree or diploma, learning a new skill, or signing up for that cooking or photography course you've always wanted to take. Reading this book, practicing mindfulness, and learning assertiveness skills are other examples of learning-related goals.

Circle yes or no for the following two questions:

yes   or   no   Is this area important to you?

yes   or   no   Does this area involve at least one of your feared social situations?

If you responded yes to both questions, please identify your values and goals for this life area.

Leisure/Recreation

This life area is about the activities you do in your free time, such as hobbies, sports, and vacations. If you are struggling with social anxiety, you may not be getting the most out of your leisure time. Perhaps you hold back your opinions at your book club, or avoid playing baseball or swimming at the local pool. Of course, there is nothing wrong with engaging in solitary pastimes (such as reading, watching television, or playing video games), if they are what you really want to do. How would you spend your free time if you were the ideal you? What matters most to you about recreation?

Circle yes or no for the following two questions:

yes   or   no   Is this area important to you?

yes   or   no   Does this area involve at least one of your feared social situations?

If you responded yes to both questions, please identify your values and goals for this life area.

Health/Physical Well-Being

This domain covers all aspects of your health and physical well-being, many of which can involve social interactions. Do you avoid shopping for healthy food, meeting with your doctor or dentist, going for walks, or joining a gym because of social fears? Do you drink alcohol, smoke, or use street drugs to manage social anxiety? If so, are your actions consistent with what you value for your health and physical well-being? What truly matters to you about your health and level of fitness? What are some health-related goals you can set for yourself?

Circle yes or no for the following two questions:

yes   or   no   Is this area important to you?

yes   or   no   Does this area involve at least one of your feared social situations?

If you responded yes to both questions, please identify your values and goals for this life area.

Community Participation

Communities can be defined in different ways, such as by location (neighborhood, apartment building, city, country, and so on), by type of group (political, ethnic, charitable, and so on), or in other ways. Has struggling with social fears kept you from volunteering at a women's shelter, sitting on your condo board, or joining a political party? How do you want to stand in relationship to the community or communities you belong to (or wish to belong to)? Examples of community-related values are being a good neighbor, protecting the environment, and providing leadership at your favorite charity. Corresponding community-related goals could include watching your neighbor's house when she is out of town, organizing a recycling drive, and leading a United Way campaign (perhaps at your place of work).

Circle yes or no for the following two questions:

yes   or   no   Is this area important to you?

yes   or   no   Does this area involve at least one of your feared social situations?

If you responded yes to both questions, please identify your values and goals for this life area.

Spirituality

This area includes organized religion and other ways of connecting to your spiritual nature, to something larger than yourself. Certain aspects of spirituality can be solitary, such as prayer, meditation, and reflection. Other aspects can be quite social and public: singing, kneeling, and reading at places of worship, as well as chatting with fellow worshippers. If spirituality is important to you, in what ways does it matter? Has struggling with social fear kept you from your spiritual goals? What are those goals?

Circle yes or no for the following two questions:

yes   or   no   Is this area important to you?

yes   or   no   Does this area involve at least one of your feared social situations?

If you responded yes to both questions, please identify your values and goals for this life area.

Other Life Areas

In the category of other life areas, you can record values and goals that don't seem to fit in any of the previous categories. An example is "Relationships with Pets." Another option is to use this category to create one or more subcategories from the life areas already covered. For example, you may want to separate "Parenting" from "Family Relationships" or create a separate category for "Mindful Living." There is no "right" or "wrong" way to categorize life areas, as long as you do it in a way that fits for you.

Next, you will find the "Values and Goals Worksheet" with examples from John and Camille, followed by a blank worksheet for you to complete.

Sample Exercise 3.2   Values and Goals Worksheet

Identify one or more values (qualities of actions), and one or more goals (outcomes of actions) for each life area that is important to you *and* involves at least one of your feared social situations.

Intimate Relationships

Values: John: *As a husband, be a loving and equal partner in child care.*

Camille: *Share my life's passions with a soul mate.*

Goals: John: *Take over some things that Dana is currently doing (like carpooling).*

Camille: *Find a partner, get married, travel the world with him.*

Friendships and Other Social Relationships

Values: John: *To be friendly, open, compassionate, and respectful toward everyone I encounter.*

Camille: *To connect deeply with friends; to listen to their dreams and challenges, and share mine; to be supportive of my friends as best I can.*

Goals: John: *Get to know neighbors, chat with other parents, make small talk with salespeople.*

Camille: *Make some like-minded friends; talk to one person at least once a day.*

Family Relationships

Values: John: *Be a great father: affectionate, a good role model, involved, consistent.*

Camille: *This area doesn't involve any of my feared situations (I do, however, value being a caring daughter, sister, and aunt).*

Goals: John: *Meet with kids' teachers, attend their games, volunteer to coach daughter's soccer team.*

Camille: *I could change a few things, but they're not related to my social fears, so I'll leave them for another time.*

Career/Employment

Values: John: *Work doesn't involve any of my feared social situations (so I won't list my career-related values here).*

Camille: *Through my career, make a lasting contribution to protecting the environment.*

Goals: John: *Not applicable (because not related to my social fears).*

Camille: *Get a new job; talk to people at a job fair.*

Education/Learning

Values: John: *Be bold; explore areas outside my comfort zone.*

Camille: *Remain open to learning about the environment.*

Goals: John: *Learn Spanish (I never was good at languages); speak with locals on our next trip to Mexico.*

Camille: *Set up a study group with friends; take a course on birds.*

Leisure/Recreation

Values: John: *To have fun and be adventurous.*

Camille: *To explore nature, hiking, and the world with like-minded others.*

Goals: John: *Ask Dana to join dancing classes with me; try out rock climbing.*

Camille: *Join a hiking group; attend seminar on bird-watching.*

Health/Physical Well-Being

Values: John: *Be a model of healthy living for my kids.*

Camille: *Physical fitness, especially good muscle strength for hiking.*

Goals: John: *Schedule checkup with my doctor; reduce drinking at social gatherings.*

Camille: *Join a gym; work out twice a week on the treadmill.*

Community Participation

Values: John: *Be a helpful, dependable neighbor and member of my community.*

Camille: *Contribute to protection of the environment through volunteer work.*

Goals: John: *Keep our property maintained according to the aesthetic of our neighborhood; offer to shovel snow for an elderly couple.*

Camille: *Attend information meeting of the local Greenpeace chapter; consider joining the chapter.*

Spirituality

Values: John: *Not an important area for me.*

Camille: *Connect with my spiritual side through meditation.*

Goals: John: *Not applicable (because not important to me).*

Camille: *Attend yearly meditation retreats in India, Thailand, and the United States.*

Other Life Areas

This category was not completed by John or Camille, because all issues important to them were covered in the previous categories.

Exercise 3.2   Values and Goals Worksheet

Identify one or more values (qualities of actions), and one or more goals (outcomes of actions) for each life area that is important to you *and* involves at least one of your feared social situations.

Intimate Relationships

Values: _____

_____

_____

Goals: _____

_____

_____

Friendships and Other Social Relationships

Values: _____

_____

_____

Goals: _____

_____

_____

Family Relationships

Values: _____

_____

_____

Goals: _____

_____

_____

Career/Employment

Values: _____

_____

_____

Goals: _____

_____

_____

Education/Learning

Values: _____

_____

_____

Goals: _____

_____

_____

Leisure/Recreation

Values: _____

_____

_____

Goals: _____

_____

_____

Health/Physical Well-Being

Values: _____

_____

_____

Goals: _____

_____

_____

Community Participation

Values: _____

_____

_____

Goals: _____

_____

_____

Spirituality

Values: _____

_____

_____

Goals: _____

_____

_____

Other Life Areas

Values: _____

_____

_____

Goals: _____

_____

_____

How did completing your "Values and Goals Worksheet" go? If you found it difficult, please keep in mind that the worksheet is meant to be an initial blueprint or work in progress, not a final document. If you have been more focused on avoiding social danger in your life than on exploring what you really want, it will take time to discover your true values and goals. There will be opportunities to add to, subtract from, and otherwise modify your worksheet later.

As we mentioned at the end of chapter 2, getting in touch with your values and goals is one of several skills you will need for shifting from the pursuit of safety to the pursuit of what truly matters in your life. In the next chapter, we introduce another of those skills: mindfulness.

CHAPTER 4

Introducing Mindfulness

In this book, we are using the following popular definition of mindfulness: "paying attention in a particular way: on purpose, in the present moment, and nonjudgmentally" (Kabat-Zinn 1994, 4). Before delving into the specifics of mindfulness, we want to share an interesting story about the impact of changing the way you pay attention.

In 2005 we both attended a talk by Jon Kabat-Zinn, who was in Toronto promoting a new book. Partway through his very engaging talk, he told the audience he was going to show a short video clip of people passing around basketballs. Our task was to watch the video and count the number of passes made by people wearing white shirts, while ignoring passes by players wearing black shirts. (You can try the task yourself before reading any further by visiting www.youtube.com/watch?v=vJG698U2Mvo&#0022;feature=player _embedded.) So it was "game on," and we watched the video with intense focus on the white-shirted players. It was a bit tricky to ignore the black-shirted players as they weaved among their white-shirted counterparts, sometimes obscuring them, but we did our best; we wanted to get the answer right! After the video finished playing, Jon asked us to raise our hands if we had seen anything unusual, but not to say anything about what we had seen. A few hands went up, but most of us sat there wondering what he was up to and when he was going to give us the correct answer! He then instructed us to watch the video again without counting passes or paying attention to anything in particular. This time, halfway into the clip, there was a collective gasp from the audience as we noticed a person dressed in a gorilla suit enter the clip from the right, stand amid the players, face the audience, beat his or her chest a few times, and then walk offscreen to the left. We were flabbergasted. How could we have missed something so obvious the first time around?

In fact, 50 percent of viewers don't see the gorilla the first time, according to psychologists Christopher Chabris and Daniel Simons, who conducted the original experiment described in their book *The Invisible Gorilla* (2010). Like others, we missed the gorilla the first time because of "the particular way" in which we were paying attention: focused on the white-shirted players (with the intention of counting passes). In contrast, when we changed our focus for the second viewing (and changed our intention), we obtained a different picture of what took place: gorilla and all!

In a similar way, changing the way you pay attention with mindfulness (and relate to your anxious feelings and thoughts) can significantly change your "picture" (experience) of social situations. We will introduce you to mindfulness with a little help from the following mindful-eating exercise (Kabat-Zinn 1990). Raisins are typically used for this exercise, but you can use any small food item that you have on hand. You can do the exercise with the audio (see the downloads at www.newharbinger.com/20801) or by reading along with the following text. (Note: In this exercise and other mindfulness exercises in the book, including the audio downloads, we use words ending in "-ing" as a way to emphasize words as guides, not commands.)

  Exercise 4.1   Mindful Eating

Start by placing a raisin in the palm of one hand.

Next, see if you can set your intention to bring a nonjudging attitude to your moment-to-moment awareness of the raisin. Whenever you lose sight of that intention during the exercise, see if you can recommit to paying mindful attention to the raisin.

Now, focus on seeing the raisin as if you've never seen one before, using your "beginner's mind"—noticing the shape, size, and color of the raisin—turning it around in your fingers, noticing the folds and where the surface reflects light, bringing an attitude of curiosity to seeing all aspects of the raisin. Whenever you notice thoughts about the raisin, such as *It's so wrinkly* or *I wish I had a bigger one,* or you notice yourself thinking about anything other than the raisin, gently redirect your attention to seeing the raisin, allowing your experience to be, exactly as it is, in this moment.

Next, focus on feeling the texture of the raisin between your fingers, noticing any softness, hardness, coarseness, smoothness, stickiness, or any other aspect of texture, simply being with your experience of feeling this raisin.

Now, holding the raisin below your nose, pay attention to smelling it, noticing the qualities of its aroma. Is it sweet, sour, musty? Is the aroma intense or faint, or is there no scent at all? If you notice your mind judging the smell, such as with thoughts like *The sweetness is lovely* or *This is too sour*, simply note the mind judging and return your focus to the pure sensation of smell.

Now, taking the raisin to one ear and rolling it between your fingers, notice any sound the raisin makes. Notice any thoughts about doing this: *This is crazy, raisins don't make sounds. Wow, I can hear the raisin.* Redirect your attention to simply hearing the raisin.

Now place the raisin in your mouth, perhaps noticing your mouth watering as you do so. Focus on the feel of the raisin in your mouth, exploring it with your tongue, noticing its shape, texture, and any initial taste. Bring your beginner's mind to the feel of the raisin in your mouth.

Now biting into the raisin, notice any flavors that are released, letting go of judgments, simply being with the taste of this raisin. As you slowly chew the raisin, pay attention to its changing consistency and the flow of saliva in your mouth.

When you first notice the urge to swallow the raisin, stay with the urge for a few moments, noticing the location and intensity of the urge, allowing it to be there as it is.

Now intentionally swallow the raisin, noticing any sensations as it passes down your throat and into your stomach.

You can repeat the exercise with another raisin or try contrasting the experience of mindful eating with how you would normally eat one or more raisins.

The Three Aspects of Mindfulness

As we check in with your experience of that exercise, let's examine each of the three parts of the definition of mindfulness: paying attention on purpose, in the present moment, and nonjudgmentally.

Paying Attention on Purpose

Mindful attention is deliberate. At the beginning of the exercise, you were invited to set your intention: to mindfully eat a raisin. What was your experience of that intention? Did you lose sight of it at any time during the exercise? When we mindfully eat raisins in the first session of our groups, some participants find it embarrassing to slowly eat a raisin in front of other people. They report that their intention to be mindful is hijacked, because their attention is drawn to signs of danger (such as experiencing shaky hands or thinking that the instructor is glancing at them), followed by urges to protect themselves from that danger (for example, *Get it over with*, *Do it right*). Other group members report that intentions to be mindful simply evaporate into "mindless" awareness, with their attention flitting about from here to there (for example, from reviewing the day to planning for tomorrow to noticing sounds and bodily sensations, and so on).

The tendency to lose sight of the intention to be mindful is very common. However, with practice, your ability to stay intentionally focused will get stronger and stronger. In the remaining chapters, you will have opportunities to practice bringing intentional focus to bodily sensations, feelings, thoughts, and, lastly, your feared social situations. In those situations, you will practice staying focused, on purpose, on what really matters. No matter how often your attention is drawn to potential social danger in those situations, you will always have the choice to redirect your focus to your valued goals.

Paying Attention in the Present Moment

Mindful attention is firmly rooted in the present: in the unfolding of your direct experience from moment to moment. (Your direct experience is that which is registered by your five senses: sight, hearing, touch, smell, and taste. Thinking about something, like a raisin, is *not* the same as directly experiencing it.)

For how much of the exercise were you able to "stay present" with your raisin? How often did your mind wander to thoughts about the raisin (*It's sweet*, *This is weird*, *Hope I don't choke*), to thoughts about other things (*What should I have for dinner tonight?*), and to awareness of unintended targets (for example, bodily sensations or sounds in the room)? What was your experience of the raisin when you *were* able to "stay present" with it? Our clients often comment that the exercise gives them the opportunity to really "know" raisins: how they look, feel, smell, sound, and taste. In the same vein, staying present to your direct experience of social situations can give you opportunities to really "know" them and to base your opinions (and actions) on that knowledge, not on what your mind tells you about the situation. For example, once Emily had gotten some practice under her belt at staying present during conversations (instead of listening to what her mind was saying about her shaky voice), she found that she rarely lost track of what others were saying, and she enjoyed conversations much more, as a result. As we proceed with additional mindfulness exercises, you will have many opportunities to practice remaining fully present to your experience. Fortunately, this will be very much facilitated by the third and final part of the mindfulness definition, paying attention nonjudgmentally.

Paying Attention Nonjudgmentally, with Acceptance

With mindful attention, we bring a nonjudging, open attitude to our experience. We also refer to this way of relating to feelings and thoughts as *acceptance*, defined as opening up to and allowing your experience to be exactly as it is, without trying to avoid it, escape it, or change it.

How did you do with remaining open to your experience of eating a raisin? Was it difficult to let go of judgments and resistance, and simply let your experience be, in the moment? If you were able to do that (for even a few seconds), what was that like? Was it perhaps liberating to gain some distance and freedom from your judging mind?

Now, perhaps you are wondering, if acceptance is part of the definition of mindfulness, why do we say mindfulness *and* acceptance (as in the title of this book)? Isn't that redundant? Yes; however, we (and others) do it to emphasize the crucial importance of the role of acceptance in this new way of relating to your thoughts and feelings. In the next section, we further explore the concept of acceptance.

Exploring Acceptance

We have found that certain metaphors are helpful in getting at the concept of acceptance, also known as *willingness*. (In fact, we have come to prefer that term, because it seems to be less easily confused with "resignation.") First, let's take a look at how acceptance is like dropping the rope in a tug of war (Hayes, Strosahl, and Wilson 1999).

Tug-of-war with Thor. Imagine that a friend asks you to take care of his dog, a mastiff named Thor that weighs two hundred pounds. Thor wants to play and brings you his rope toy for a game of tug-of-war. You pick up one end of the rope with both hands, and Thor has the other end in a death grip in his powerful jaws. As he pulls, Thor is growling and has that crazed look in his eyes that signals his intention to hang on indefinitely. Each time you pull, Thor pulls back even harder. He won't let go, and you're stuck there using your entire body to keep from being pulled over, similar to the way your struggle with anxious feelings and thoughts can consume much of your time and energy. However, if you drop the rope, you are freed up to do whatever you want. Thor is still there and may try to get you to pick up the rope again to continue the game, but it's your choice whether or not to do that. In a similar vein, when you "drop the rope" in your struggle with anxious thoughts and feelings, when you are willing to have your experience as it is, you are freed up to live the life you really want. However, just because you are willing to "have" your anxiety doesn't mean you "want" it, as is demonstrated in the next metaphor about welcoming an unwanted guest (Hayes, Strosahl, and Wilson 1999).

Welcoming Uncle Leo. Imagine having spent a year planning your dream wedding, carefully attending to every detail, including the guest list. You chose not to invite Uncle Leo, because he can be surly, has poor hygiene, and never dresses properly. You didn't want to risk having him spoil your day. Finally, the big day arrives and everything is going according to plan. You are on the dance floor for your first dance, when you see Uncle Leo standing by the bar. But you don't *want* him there! Well, you could leave the dance floor, escort him to a cab, and spend the rest of the evening scanning the room, ready to escort him out again if he dares to return. But then, of course, you wouldn't be able to enjoy your own wedding. Or, you could welcome Uncle Leo, make room for him at a table, and get back to tearing up the dance floor. You still don't want him there, but you are willing to allow him to stay so that you can fully participate in one of the most important days of your life. Similarly, just as you don't want your anxious thoughts and feelings, you can still be willing to allow their existence so that you can be a full participant on your social-anxiety playing field. Finally, we want to point out that willingness is like a switch. (We got the idea for the "willingness switch" from Russ Harris's "struggle switch," described in his excellent book, *The Happiness Trap* 2008.)

The willingness switch. We often ask people to rate their anxiety level on a scale from 0 to 10, where 0 represents no anxiety and 10 represents the worst anxiety they've ever experienced. Now it might make sense that willingness could also be rated in a similar way, with 0 representing no willingness (or complete unwillingness) and 10 representing complete willingness to experience anxiety. You could think of willingness as being like a dimmer switch on a light that you can turn from low to high and everything in between. However, the problem with looking at willingness as a dimmer switch is that only the 10 setting is free of resistance. At a setting of 8, you may be "resigned to" your experience, at 6 "tolerating" it, at 4 "grinning and bearing" it, at 2 "white-knuckling" your anxious thoughts and feelings (or whichever expressions fit for you), but only at 10 are you allowing them to come and go as they will.

Instead of as a dimmer switch, we like to think of willingness as a switch that has only two positions, off and on. When your willingness switch is off, you are caught up in a struggle with your experience, whether that consists of just a little struggle or a whole lot of struggle. However, when your willingness switch is flipped on, you are completely open to your experience, allowing it to be exactly as it is. In upcoming exercises, we will invite you to "flip on your willingness switch" as you practice bringing an attitude of acceptance and allowing to your anxious feelings and thoughts on your social-anxiety playing field. If that sounds daunting, don't worry; you get to choose certain details: exactly what you will do with your willingness switch on, for how long, and under which circumstances (for example, *I will talk to my neighbor Sam for two minutes, only if he's alone*).

As you practice willingness in upcoming exercises, you may find it helpful to use these three metaphors, reminding yourself to "drop the rope," "welcome Uncle Leo," and "flip on your willingness switch," as you let go of your struggle with anxious thoughts and feelings, and make room for your experience. Along with those metaphors, another way to facilitate acceptance is to get in touch with your observer perspective.

The Observer Perspective

The *observer perspective* is simply the part of your mind that notices things: feelings, thoughts, sights, sounds, and so on. You use it all day long without having much awareness of it. However, you can recruit it to help you in observing your experience with openness and acceptance, from the stance of an impartial witness. We find it helpful to get in touch with the observer perspective through the use of certain images, such as a mountain. The following exercise, the "Observing Mountain," was adapted from Jon Kabat-Zinn's mountain meditation (1994) with permission.

We invite you to get in touch with your observing mountain by listening to the audio for the following exercise (see the audio downloads at www.newharbinger.com/20801) or by going through the following written text.

 ## Exercise 4.2   The Observing Mountain

This exercise is best done while seated on a chair or mat, but can also be done lying down. Start by getting into a comfortable position and allowing your eyes to close gently. Then take a few moments to come into the present moment by connecting with your breathing, noticing each full in-breath and each full out-breath.

Now, bring to mind the image of a mountain, perhaps a mountain you have visited or seen in photographs, or one of your own imagination. Bring into focus as many details of this mountain as possible. Imagine its size and shape. Perhaps it's a snow-covered peak with trees and meadows on its lower slopes. Notice that your mountain, like all mountains, has a solid, unmoving base.

However the mountain appears, just sitting and breathing with the image of this mountain, observing it and noting its qualities. And when you feel ready, see if you can bring the mountain into your own body, so that your body and the mountain become one. Perhaps your head is the mountain's peak, your shoulders and arms are the sides of the mountain, and your bottom and legs are its solid base. With each breath you become a little more the mountain—solid, still, and centered.

And, as you connect with the solid core of your mountain, can you also observe its surface, noticing the multitude of changes that take place on it, from day to day, and season to season? As day turns to night, perhaps noticing how the temperature drops, and the light gradually fades. In spring, perhaps you can feel a gentle rain, or see dense fog obscuring the view. In summer, meadows may be filled with wildflowers, mountain goats graze in the warmth of the sun, or forest fires may ravage the surface. In winter, you may watch as snow falls softly on stately evergreens, or avalanches destroy everything in their paths. You may also notice people on your mountain voicing their differing opinions of it—it is the best or worst mountain they have seen, or it is too easy or too difficult to climb. And, as you observe all of these changes on the surface of your mountain, can you also realize that its solid base remains unchanged?

Perhaps at times, on your social-anxiety playing field, you can connect with your inner mountain, embodying its strength and stability, observing your inner experiences as you would the ever-changing surface of a mountain. And realize, as you notice your thoughts and feelings come and go, that your essential self—your core—remains unchanged.

What was your experience of that exercise? We are particularly fond of the mountain image because of the sense of stability and strength it conveys. However, it may not resonate for you, and that's fine. Next, we describe two additional images that can be helpful in connecting with your observer perspective.

The lake image. Imagine the inner core of your body as the still depths of a lake; from your "inner lake," you can observe your thoughts and feelings, just as you would the waves, boats, ice, leaves, and other "disturbances" on the surface of a lake (Kabat-Zinn 1994).

The train-track image. Imagine your arms and legs as the solid steel rails of a train track. From your "inner train track," you can observe your thoughts and feelings, as you would the passing of loudly clanking cars.

When you are trying out the lake and train-track images, take a few moments to settle into a lying-down position (sitting is also okay) before bringing one of the images to mind. From the perspective of your "inner lake" or "inner train track," take five to ten minutes to simply notice and watch as your feelings and thoughts come and go. In later chapters, we will ask you to try connecting with your observer perspective in your feared social situations. Doing this can often create a little distance between you and your anxious feelings and thoughts, making it easier to observe them with acceptance and compassion.

Perhaps you can think of other images that might be helpful in connecting more deeply with your observer perspective. Record them here: _____

_____

_____

We recommend that you try out "The Observing Mountain" exercise (with or without audio) and the other observer images over the next several weeks. You can record your observations in the following Mindfulness Log, which can be used for all of the mindfulness exercises in this book (except for the "abs" exercises; see chapter 5).

Mindfulness Log

Day	Mindfulness Activity	Observations
Monday		
Tuesday		
Wednesday		
Thursday		
Friday		
Saturday		
Sunday		

Additional Notes on Mindfulness

In this book, we concentrate on the benefits of paying mindful attention on your social-anxiety playing field. Although we encourage you to practice "off your field" (that is, outside of your feared social situations, perhaps as you are relaxing at home on a weekend), the goal of that practice is to assist you in developing your capacity to more readily access mindfulness "on your field" (that is, in your feared social situations). However, you may certainly find that there are other situations where paying mindful attention can be beneficial. In our own lives, we practice mindfulness for pain, to enhance parenting, and for other reasons. (For additional resources about mindfulness, please see appendix B.)

As you continue to work through the book, we recommend that you practice paying mindful attention to routine daily activities (such as eating) for five to ten minutes per day. Other daily activities might include taking a shower, brushing your teeth, and doing household chores (such as washing the dishes or taking out the trash). As you practice intentionally bringing an open, present-moment focus to your direct experience of these activities, be sure to pay attention (as you did with the raisin) to what you see, hear, smell, taste, and touch (where relevant). You can also practice paying attention to one sense at a time (for example, being mindful of "seeing" a sunset, "hearing" the symphony, "smelling" at a bakery, "tasting" at a restaurant, and "touching" as you fold the laundry). If you do that, try to focus on "pure" sensation, as described in the following mindful seeing and hearing exercises (based on Segal, Williams, and Teasdale 2002).

Exercise 4.3 Mindful Seeing

Start by choosing a location for this exercise. You can practice mindful seeing in nature, at work, at home, as you're walking down the street, or in any location, for that matter. (With our clients, we usually do this exercise standing at a window in an office, paying mindful attention to the sights outside.) Set aside a few minutes to simply "see" what there is to be seen in your chosen location. Try letting go of the categories you normally use to make sense of what you are seeing. Rather than labeling what you see (as a tree, person, car, squirrel, and so on), simply notice patterns of color, shape, and movement. Try focusing on a very small feature in your field of vision, and then spread your awareness out to the whole field of vision. Whenever thoughts of what you are seeing come to mind, simply notice them and gently bring your attention back to pure sensations of seeing. In many instances (such as in nature, when viewing sunsets, and so on), you may find that mindful seeing enhances your experience of the setting.

Exercise 4.4   Mindful Hearing

Start by choosing a location for this exercise. You can practice mindful hearing at home, at work, at a concert, in nature, or in any location, for that matter. Set aside a few minutes to simply "hear" what there is to be heard in the location you have chosen. Bring your attention to sounds as they arise, wherever they arise: sounds that are close, sounds that are far away, and the silences between sounds. As best you can, be aware of sounds as simply pure sensation—noticing patterns of pitch, tone, volume, and duration—letting go of the urge to label what you are hearing (such as a voice, bird, guitar, footsteps, and so on). There is no need to go searching for sounds or to listen for particular sounds. Whenever you find that you are thinking about sounds, reconnect as best you can with pure hearing. In some settings (such as listening to music, birds singing, and so on), mindful hearing can enhance your experience.

Over the next few weeks, try out mindful seeing and mindful hearing in a number of different locations. You can also try alternating between mindful seeing and mindful hearing in the same location (devoting a period of time, from a few seconds to a few minutes, to each "sense"). Be sure to record your observations in your "Mindfulness Log."

Now that you have an overview of mindfulness, we are going to focus more specifically on bringing mindfulness skills to your anxious feelings. In the next chapter, we help you to strengthen your "abs"!

CHAPTER 5

Strengthening Your "Abs": Acceptance of Bodily Sensations

In earlier chapters, we saw that Emily, Jack, and Camille all experienced physical sensations of anxiety, as do many socially anxious people. In all of their cases, resisting their anxious feelings led them to avoid doing things that really mattered to them—such as making friends (Emily), attending job interviews (Camille), and speaking up at meetings (Jack)—which kept them from living the lives they truly wanted.

The following "Niagara Falls" metaphor (based on the polygraph metaphor from Hayes, Strosahl, and Wilson 1999) is about the difficulty of trying to control anxious feelings. Imagine that you're in a helicopter flying over Niagara Falls. You're in a seat that has been fitted with very special anxiety sensors. If it picks up even a hint of fear, you will be ejected from the seat into the falls below, to an almost certain death. Under those circumstances, would you remain safely in your seat? Having visited these massively powerful falls many times, we both know that we wouldn't last more than a second in the helicopter seat, even with our lives at stake. In a similar vein, have you noticed that just when it seems most important to you to control your anxiety in your feared social situations is when it's most difficult? As discussed earlier in the book, an alternative to controlling and resisting feelings is to accept them.

In this chapter, we outline a three-pronged, gradual approach that you can use to build up your willingness to experience physical sensations of anxiety. This approach involves a series of exercises for strengthening your "abs": your *acceptance of bodily sensations*. The exercises are all about paying mindful attention to your body: first, to your body in stillness; second, to your body in movement; and finally, to your body as you intentionally bring on anxious bodily sensations. The aim of this approach is to gradually cultivate your capacity to open up to, and let go of, your struggle with physical sensations of anxiety. At each step of the way, as your willingness switch grows stronger and stronger, you will find that you have more time and energy for pursuing your valued goals.

Paying Mindful Attention to Your Body in Stillness

The first exercise, the "body scan," involves bringing mindful attention to different parts of the body in turn (Kabat-Zinn 1990). You can scan the body slowly (over thirty to forty-five minutes) or quickly (over a few minutes), depending on the time you have available. Our version of the body scan lasts about fifteen minutes (on the accompanying audio available for download at www.newharbinger.com/20801). We invite you to try it now.

  ## Exercise 5.1   Body Scan

The intention of this practice is to bring mindful awareness to sensations in the body as you focus your attention systematically on each part of the body in turn. It is to be aware of your experience as it is unfolding, however it is. Not to change the way you are feeling or to become more relaxed or calmer.

First, making yourself comfortable lying on your back, in a place where you will be warm and undisturbed. Lying on a mat, a rug, the floor, or a bed. Lying with palms open to the ceiling, feet falling apart from each other, and eyes gently closed. As best you can, keeping still during the exercise, but if you need to move or adjust your position, doing so mindfully, with complete awareness.

So to begin, just becoming aware of breathing. Taking the attention to the abdomen, noting it rise with the in-breath and fall with the out-breath. Not trying to manipulate the breath in any way, just experiencing it as it is, as it moves in and out of the body. Full attention in each moment to breathing.

And on the next out-breath, moving your awareness down your body to the toes of both the left foot and the right foot, and noticing whatever sensations are present in the toes. Perhaps noticing warmth, coolness, tingling, moisture, itching, whatever is arising from the toes, whether there are sensations or no sensations. Being aware of the big toes and the little toes and the toes in between.

And on the next out-breath, letting go of your toes in your mind's eye and moving your attention to the rest of the feet. To the tops of both feet. The soles of both feet, and the ankles. Just staying open to whatever sensations you find there. And if there are no sensations, that is just fine.

And on the next out-breath, letting go of the awareness of the feet, and shifting the focus of attention to the lower legs. Becoming aware of the calves, perhaps noting where they touch the floor or the mat. Becoming aware of the shins, the skin over the legs, and just being attentive to this part of your body.

And on the next out-breath, allowing the lower legs to dissolve in your mind's eye as you move gently with your attention to the knees. Becoming aware of the part under the knee, and on top of the knee, perhaps being aware of what a complex joint the knee is, with tendons and ligaments and the kneecap. And just being here with your knees, letting them predominate in your field of awareness, in the moment. And now gently releasing the knees and moving your attention to the thighs. Noticing whatever sensations arise in the left thigh and the right thigh. And if your mind has wandered, just gently and kindly bringing your attention back to the thighs.

And on the next out-breath, letting go of awareness of the thighs as you bring your attention to the pelvic region. To the buttocks, the tailbone, the pelvic bone, the genitals. Staying open to whatever sensations you find, just being attentive to this part of your body.

And on the next out-breath, letting go of the awareness of the pelvic region and moving your attention to the abdomen. Bringing a gentle curiosity and openness to whatever you find in this moment. Perhaps noticing a gentle rise of the abdomen with the in-breath and the fall of the abdomen with the out-breath.

And on the next out-breath, letting go of the abdomen in your mind's eye and moving your attention to the chest area, the area that contains your heart and lungs. Perhaps noticing the beating of your heart or the expansion of the rib cage as you breathe in. Staying open to whatever sensations you find in the chest.

And on the next out-breath, letting go of the chest in your mind's eye as you bring your attention to the lower back. A part of the body that often carries a lot of tension. Just noticing whatever sensations arise, whether there be tension or no tension and not trying to make it be any different, just accepting the sensations that are there. Letting go of the tendency we all have to want things to be different.

And on the next out-breath, letting go of the awareness of the lower back and bringing your awareness to the upper back, the back ribs, and the shoulder blades. Another area where the body holds tension. And just being with the upper back, not going anywhere or doing anything but developing an openness to all that is arising from this part of the body. And as thoughts arise, just being present for thoughts and then returning to paying attention to the upper back.

And on the next out-breath, letting go of the upper back in your mind's eye as you move gently with your attention to the hands. Becoming aware of the fingers, the palms, the backs of the hands, and the wrists. Becoming aware of any sensations arising in the hands. Perhaps warmth, or coolness, tingling or moisture. Just bringing a compassionate awareness to whatever arises in the hands.

And on the next out-breath, letting go of the hands in the mind's eye and moving your attention to the arms. To the lower arms, the elbows, and the upper arms. Bringing a gentle curiosity and openness to whatever you find in this moment. And now gently releasing the arms and shifting the focus of attention to the neck. Noticing whatever sensations arise in the neck. And if your mind has wandered, gently and kindly bringing your attention back to the neck.

And on the next out-breath, letting go of awareness of the neck, as you bring your awareness to the face and the rest of the head. Becoming aware of the jaw, the mouth, the nose, the cheeks, the ears, the eyes, the forehead, the scalp, and the back and top of the head. Noticing whatever sensations arise in the face and the head. Just noticing without judgment. There is no right way to feel when you are doing this. The way you feel is the way you feel.

And on the next out-breath, letting go of awareness of the face and the head. And now, taking a few deep breaths, breathing in through the nose, and allowing the breath to move through the body to the tips of your toes, and then allowing the breath to move up from your toes, through your body, as you exhale through the nose. And doing this a few times, breathing in all the way through the body to the toes and back out through the nose.

And now letting go of the awareness of breathing and getting a sense of the body as whole and complete. Resting in this state of openness to things as they are.

As we practice the body scan, we develop the capacity to just observe our sensations and work at letting them be as they are, without reacting. We come to see from our own experience that we don't have to struggle with our thoughts, physical sensations, and feelings or force them to be different. And now, perhaps, making the intention of taking this attitude of acceptance and openness with you through the rest of your day.

What was your experience of the body scan? Some people find it so relaxing that they fall asleep. If that happened to you, try keeping your eyes open when you repeat the exercise, or do it while seated or standing (instead of lying down). Others find that sensations of tension and pain are intensified during the exercise, and they have difficulty with bringing an accepting attitude to those uncomfortable feelings. If that was your experience during the exercise, it is important to be patient and compassionate with yourself. If you are like most people, this is a very new way of approaching uncomfortable feelings, very different from our usual tendency to judge and resist pain and discomfort. It will take practice to cultivate this new approach. (At the end of the chapter, we suggest a schedule for practicing the body scan and other "abs" exercises, and we include a form for recording your observations.)

Paying Mindful Attention to Your Body in Movement

Next, to build on the practice of the body scan, let's move on to paying mindful attention to your body as it moves through a series of gentle stretches. The second exercise, "Mindful Stretching," includes some of the common yoga positions described by Kabat-Zinn (1990). It is best to do this exercise with the audio (see the audio downloads at www.newharbinger. com/20801); it might be helpful to first read the following transcript of the exercise to get a sense of what to expect with the audio version, perhaps trying out some of the stretches before following along with the audio.

  ## Exercise 5.2 Mindful Stretching

The intention of this exercise is to bring mindful awareness, as best you can, to physical sensations throughout the body as we proceed through a series of gentle stretches. With each stretch it is important to notice the limits of your body and, as best you can, try to let go of any tendency to push beyond your limits or to compete with yourself. If a particular stretch is too challenging for your body at any time, simply maintain the standing position or repeat an earlier stretch.

So to begin, standing in bare feet or socks on the floor, a mat, or a rug, with the feet about hip-width apart, knees unlocked and feet parallel to each other.

And becoming aware of the flow of the breath, paying complete attention to each full in-breath and each full out-breath, not controlling the breath in any way.

And then taking a few moments to feel the body as a whole, from head to toe, perhaps noticing the sensations in the feet as they make contact with the floor or mat or rug.

Now, on an in-breath, slowly and mindfully raising the arms out to the sides, parallel to the floor, now breathing out, and on the next in-breath, continuing to raise the arms until they meet above the head, feeling any tension in the muscles as they work to lift the arms and maintain them in the stretch. And as you hold the stretch, noticing any sensations, perhaps warmth or tingling, bringing a gentle curiosity to whatever you find. And when the mind wanders, as it surely will, just noting that and redirecting your attention to the body stretching in this position.

And then on an out-breath, very slowly bringing the arms down and letting them hang at the sides of the body. Then repeating that stretch, raising the arms out to the side, then meeting above the head, holding, then returning very slowly to the sides.

And allowing the eyes to close gently and noticing how it feels to have just done that stretch. And after a few breaths, opening the eyes again.

Now stretching just the right arm above the head, and letting the heel of the left foot lift off the floor, as the right arm reaches toward the ceiling. With full awareness of any sensations in the body. And then letting the right arm drop back to the side and the left heel touch the ground, and raising the left arm above the head, reaching up and stretching the fingers toward the ceiling, with the right heel raised off the floor, noticing whatever sensations arise with this stretch, perhaps becoming aware of any difference in sensations from when you did it with the right arm. Then letting the left arm drop back to the side and the right heel touch the ground, returning to standing with both feet flat on the ground, arms resting at the sides.

And then repeating the stretch, first the right arm lifting and stretching, left foot raised, holding, then lowering the right arm and left heel, then left arm raised and reaching up, right heel lifted, holding, then returning to standing with both feet flat on the ground, arms resting at the sides.

Now raising both arms above the head, knees slightly bent, and bending at the waist, all the way over until the head hangs down, fingers pointing toward the floor, allowing them to rest wherever it's comfortable, not pushing the body in any way. And just noticing what sensations arise when the body is bending in this way. Then slowly uncurling the body, one vertebra at a time, with the head coming up last to a standing position. And now repeating that, arms above the head, knees slightly bent, bending at the waist, head hanging down, fingers pointing toward the floor, then slowly uncurling to a standing position.

Now moving the right ear toward the right shoulder as far as it will comfortably go, then taking it back up, and moving the left ear toward the left shoulder and then up. And repeating that.

Then bending the head forward, chin toward the chest and rolling the head to the left, to the back, to the right, and back to the front again. Then rolling it in the other direction, first toward the chest then to the right, to the back, left, back to the front, and up again. Then rolling the head in both directions again.

Now raising the arms to the side, parallel to the floor, and lifting the right leg out to the side, and holding it wherever it feels comfortable, just standing, perhaps noticing the focus required to stay balanced. And also noticing any thoughts, particularly about not doing this right, and letting go of thoughts as you keep the attention on this position. Now lowering the right leg and allowing the arms to fall to the side and standing for a moment with eyes closed. Now raising the arms to the side again, parallel to the floor, and lifting the left leg out to the side, and holding it wherever it feels comfortable, not pushing your limits. Perhaps noticing any wobbling or shaking, which are normal when balancing on one leg. And then lowering the left leg and allowing the arms to fall to the side and standing for a moment with eyes closed. And now repeating that stretch, first with the right leg and then the left.

Now, with the left foot turned out at a 45-degree angle, moving the right leg forward, and bending the right knee into a lunge, left leg stretched out straight behind, and reaching the arms above the head, holding this stretch, paying mindful attention to any sensations in the body, not needing them to be any different than they are, in this moment. Then pushing back up with the right foot and leg to a standing position. Then, with the right foot turned out at a 45-degree angle, stepping forward with the left leg into a lunge, bending the left knee, right leg stretched out straight behind, and raising the arms above the head, and holding in this position. Then pushing back up with the left foot and leg to a standing position. Now repeating this lunge on both sides. And then resting in a standing position, eyes gently closed, taking the attention to the breath, each full in-breath and each full out-breath. Full awareness of breathing. And perhaps noticing any differences in how the body feels now compared to the start of the exercise. Remembering that there is no right way or wrong way to feel. Just bringing an attitude of curiosity and compassion to whatever you find in this moment.

What was your experience of mindful stretching? Some people comment that they find areas of tension that they never knew existed and that it feels good to stretch out those tight muscles. Others find themselves caught up in thoughts about "not doing it right." In our groups, many participants are self-conscious about doing the stretches in front of others. We use this as an opportunity to practice noticing and letting go of judging thoughts, and returning to our intended focus. As with the body scan, it is important to be kind to yourself as you practice this new way of approaching bodily sensations.

Paying Mindful Attention to Your Bodily Sensations of Anxiety

The third and final "prong" of the approach for strengthening your "abs" is about paying mindful attention to your body as you purposely bring on bodily sensations of anxiety. We do this to practice "being with" these sensations with an attitude of willingness. Now, if the mere thought of intentionally causing yourself discomfort makes you nervous, join the crowd! About 90 percent of our clients are initially wary of trying this final part of the "abs" approach. However, as with our clients, we will not ask you to "jump into the deep end of the pool." We will show you how to "wade in" and go at your own pace.

Bringing on Bodily Sensations of Anxiety

The following table includes suggested actions for bringing on eleven specific bodily sensations of anxiety. After you look them over, we will show you how to use them whenever you go through the "Being with Your Anxiety" exercise that we will introduce later.

Bodily Sensations of Anxiety	Suggested Actions
Sweating or flushing	Put on heavy clothing, cover up in blankets, or both, and then turn up the temperature in your home (if possible, or use a space heater); or sit in a sauna at the gym until you start to sweat or notice flushing.

Bodily Sensations of Anxiety	Suggested Actions
Blushing	This can be a tough one to bring on. One possibility is to imagine a situation that you suspect will bring on blushing (such as noticing that you had food in your teeth throughout a conversation and so on). Also, if one of your concerns about blushing is appearing red in the face, you can try bringing that on with the previous suggestions for sweating (your face may turn red when it's warm).
Trembling	Grip a glass or other object tightly, until your hand starts to tremble; hold a push-up until your arms start to tremble; balance on one leg until it starts to tremble.
Dry mouth	Put absorbent material in your mouth to soak up any saliva; the rolls that your dentist uses would work well.
Palpitations	Run in place until you notice your heart racing; step up and down repeatedly on stairs or an exercise step.
Muscle tension	Hold a push-up position or tense all your muscles until you notice tension (often after about one minute).
Blurry vision	Stare at a light for about one minute and then read a paragraph.
Trouble swallowing	Swallow quickly about four times; apply pressure to your throat for about one minute.
Shortness of breath (breathlessness)	Stand up and breathe deeply through your mouth for about one minute; hold your breath for about thirty seconds; breathe through a small straw with your nose plugged for one to two minutes.
Dizziness or vertigo	Shake your head back and forth for about thirty seconds; lay your head on your knees and sit back up repeatedly for about thirty seconds (head lifts); spin in a chair for about one minute, or just stand and spin around (then stand still without holding on to anything).
Feelings of unreality	Stare at a spot for about two minutes, stare at your hand for about three minutes, or stare at yourself in the mirror for about two minutes.

Other sensations not previously listed	Record these sensations and your suggestions for bringing them on:
	_____

The list of suggested actions is by no means exhaustive; you are welcome to try other things that you think might be helpful in bringing on certain bodily sensations. If you have a health condition (for example, asthma, high or low blood pressure, heart disease, or a pain condition) or are pregnant, you may want to check with your doctor before trying the suggested actions. It is always important to be mindful of any physical limitations with these activities.

Exercise 5.3   Being with Your Anxiety

There are five basic steps to follow each time you go through this "Being with Your Anxiety" exercise. (Note: each time you try out a specific action, it is considered a separate "session" of the exercise.)

1. Choose relevant bodily sensations and suggested actions. Each time you go through this exercise, we recommend choosing bodily sensations that you tend to struggle with on your social-anxiety playing field. Once you have chosen a sensation to work with, you may need to experiment with the suggested actions from the previous table to see which one (if any) brings it on and how long you need to do the action to bring on the sensation. Often, increasing the duration of the suggested actions will increase the intensity of sensations. Note that some suggested actions may bring on more than one sensation (for example, deep breathing can bring on shortness of breath, palpitations, and dizziness).

2. Set your intention. Start by setting your intention to "flip on your willingness switch," to stay fully present to your direct experience of bodily sensations during the exercise.

3. Pay mindful attention during the exercise. As you do the exercise, pay mindful attention: opening up and making room for all aspects of your experience, and letting go of thoughts about it and urges to change it and control it. Two suggestions for maintaining that stance of willingness are:

Be a friendly scientist. Pay attention to your experience as if you were a friendly scientist encountering a new phenomenon: observing it with curiosity and trying to learn as much about it as you can, such as where the sensations start and end, their quality, intensity, and duration. Explore any urges to control, escape, or avoid your experience; what do *they* feel like?

Make use of metaphors. If your willingness switch flips off during an exercise and you start to resist your experience, try "dropping the rope" in your struggle with uncomfortable feelings, or try welcoming your sensations in the same way that you would "welcome Uncle Leo to the wedding." However, if your willingness switch flips off, that's fine; it's okay to stop the exercise. As mentioned in the previous chapter, you get to decide how long to keep your willingness switch flipped on. With repeated practice, your switch will gradually strengthen, and you will be able to keep it on for longer and longer periods.

4. End the exercise. As mentioned before, you can stop an exercise at any time if your willingness switch flips off. Otherwise, keep paying mindful attention to your experience until the intensity of your bodily sensations has returned to baseline (the level where it was before you started the exercise).

5. Record the exercise. When you finish an exercise, record your observations on the following "Abs Recording Form," including comments about what you might do differently the next time (for example, do it for less time, or more; try a different action to bring on sensations).

Now, take five to ten minutes to try out the "Being with Your Anxiety" exercise with one of the suggested actions on your own, noting your observations on the following recording form. (As mentioned earlier in the chapter, you can also use the recording form for the "Body Scan" and "Mindful Stretching" exercises. Whenever you do the "Being with Your Anxiety" exercise, be sure to note the sensations you targeted and how you brought them on. We recommend that you download the form at www.newharbin ger.com/20801 and keep it handy.)

Acceptance of Bodily Sensations (Abs) Recording Form

Date	Abs Exercise *	Observations
	Example: "Being with your anxiety"-dizziness-spin in chair for 30 seconds	Example: dizziness wasn't very intense; try 45 seconds next time.

* Abs Exercise: Body Scan, Mindful Stretching, Being with your Anxiety. Be sure to record sensation(s) targeted and action(s) used for "Being with your Anxiety" exercises.

What was your experience of the "Being with Your Anxiety" exercise? Were you able to bring on the intended bodily sensations and willingly experience them? Some people find that this type of exercise is not as helpful as they would like for it to be, because their main concern is about other people observing and judging their anxious sensations—and that doesn't happen when you are doing the exercises alone at home! If that's the case for you, stay tuned for suggestions in chapter 8 for doing these exercises in your feared social situations. Other people find that for some of the exercises, they can't get their willingness switches to flip on at all. If that happens for you, we recommend a more gradual approach. For example, if you don't feel ready to "willingly" breathe through a small straw with your nose plugged for one minute, try using a straw with a larger-sized tube. Start by breathing through it with your nose plugged for a few seconds, and gradually increase that duration until you can willingly do the exercise for one or two minutes. Then, you can repeat that process using a smaller straw, if you wish.

Now that you have tried all three exercises for strengthening your abs, it's important to practice them. For the next fourteen days, we suggest that you do the "Body Scan" and "Mindful Stretching" exercises on alternate days, and fit in at least one session of the "Being with Your Anxiety" exercise daily, as summarized in the following table.

Schedule of Practice for Acceptance of Bodily Sensations (Abs) Exercises

Day (in a fourteen-day period)	"Body Scan"	"Mindful Stretching"	"Being with Your Anxiety"
1 and 8	√		√
2 and 9		√	√
3 and 10	√		√
4 and 11		√	√
5 and 12	√		√
6 and 13		√	√
7 and 14	√		√

If you work on gradually strengthening your "abs," as outlined in this chapter, you will find that you have more and more time and energy to devote to your values and goals. In the next chapter, we introduce another skill for helping you to shift out of safety mode on your social-anxiety playing field: *defusion*.

CHAPTER 6

Defusing from Your Anxious Thoughts

Emily treated the thought *They think I'm weird* as if she literally were weird, so she decided not to approach anyone at the office party. For Jack, the mere thought of speaking up at the meeting was accompanied by palpitations, as if he were actually speaking, so he chose to say nothing. These examples demonstrate that when you take your thoughts literally (as facts) or fuse with them (as introduced in chapter 2), they appear to have authority, as if they were spoken by a big monster, one so powerful that you have no choice but to act on his orders if you want to keep safe. This is depicted in the illustration below, where the fused mind is directing the driver away from the path of his values, toward a path of avoidance.

Fusion: Your anxious thoughts send you down the path of avoidance.

On the other hand, when you are *defused from* your thoughts, you see them for what they are: a collection of words and images in your mind. This reduces their power, giving you the freedom to choose how to respond to them. In the second illustration, which depicts defusion, the driver is choosing the path of his values and is taking his anxious thoughts along for the ride. They are still shouting orders at him, but he has chosen not to obey them.

In this chapter, you will take a close look at your anxious thinking, and learn how to apply a wide range of defusion strategies to your fused mind. As you gain experience in unhooking from your anxious thoughts, you will develop the ability to allow your direct experience of social situations to guide your actions, instead of letting your bossy thoughts do so. Or, as noted in the title of the very first ACT self-help book, you'll gain the ability to *Get Out of Your Mind and Into Your Life* (Hayes 2005).

To start, it will be helpful for you to know a little more about your anxious thinking, beginning with some of the thoughts that typically show up in your top three feared social situations (which you identified in chapter 1). Keep a copy of your responses to the following exercise handy, because we will refer back to them as we go along.

Defusion: You can choose the path toward your values and take your anxious thoughts along for the ride.

Exercise 6.1 Your Anxious Thoughts

List some of the thoughts that typically show up in each of your top three feared social situations. Leave the "Types of Anxious Thinking" column blank for now.

Situation	Thoughts	Types of Anxious Thinking
1		
2		
3		

Types of Anxious Thinking

In this section, we will outline the most common types of thinking the socially anxious mind engages in. Others have also noted socially anxious thinking styles (for example, Antony and Swinson 2008). We are all familiar with basic types of anxious thinking, such as worrying (*I won't fit in*), having anxious memories (*It's just like that awful speech I gave in seventh grade*), evaluating or judging (*This isn't going very well, You look like an idiot*), and making negative comparisons (*He's way more interesting than I am*), to name a few. Other, slightly more elaborate types of thinking the socially anxious mind favors include the following.

Fortune-Telling

Fortune-telling is when your mind predicts what will happen, usually something negative, like *I won't have anything to say, I'll have a panic attack and won't be able to speak*, and *My coworkers will discover that I'm incompetent*.

Mind Reading

Mind reading is when your mind tells you what others are thinking about you, usually in the form of judgmental thoughts. It's easy to pick up mind reading when you notice thoughts starting with *He thinks...*, *She thinks...*, or *They think...* (for example, *She must think I'm a nervous wreck* or *They think I'm stupid and boring*).

"Shoulding"

Using statements that include the word "should," otherwise known as "shoulding" (Ellis 1994), is a popular activity of the socially anxious mind. Do any of the following "should" phrases sound familiar?

- *I shouldn't appear anxious.*

- *I should be perfect.*

- *I shouldn't inconvenience others.*

- *I should always be in control.*

- *I should always be funny and charming.*

- *I should/shouldn't* (fill in others that apply to you): _____

_____

Postmortem

Postmortem is when your mind rehashes or ruminates about what you think happened (or should have happened) in a social situation. Your "postmortem" review of a situation can last from seconds to hours, often "rearing its ugly head" from time to time long after you have left a situation. The following is an example of a "postmortem" review that Jack engaged in after he gave a presentation at work:

Oh no, I really screwed up that presentation. I should have prepared more. I can't believe I made that stupid comment about finances. And I forgot to mention the plan I've been preparing. What an idiot! The boss sure had a disappointed look on her face. I bet she regrets promoting me. I'm going to get fired, and I'll never get another job!

The Spotlight Effect

Sam worked in a hospital lab and was required to demonstrate various techniques to medical students. He told us that during demonstrations, he always felt as if he were the center of attention, as if a spotlight were shining on his shaky hands for everyone to see (and judge him about). He would often call in sick on "demo days" or beg one of his colleagues to take his place. The type of experience that Sam told us about is actually called *the spotlight effect*, as described by psychologists Thomas Gilovich and Kenneth Savitsky (1999, 165) using this humorous account of a scene from the movie *The Lonely Guy*, starring Steve Martin:

Steve Martin arrives at a restaurant and is asked by the maître d', "How many in your party, sir?" When Martin replies that he is dining alone, the maître d' raises his voice and asks with astonishment, "Alone?" The restaurant falls silent as everyone stares at

Martin in disbelief. To make matters worse, a spotlight suddenly appears from nowhere and follows Martin as he is escorted to his seat.

When we told Sam that story about the spotlight effect, he was relieved to know that his experience of painfully self-conscious thinking is common enough to show up in a popular movie!

Generating Stories

We finish this section with one final activity of the socially anxious mind: generating stories about who you are in social situations, sometimes pretty negative stories (for example, a story about you as a loser). To try to get at some of your stories, complete the following phrases:

In social situations I feel as if I am (for example, *an imposter*) _____

_____.

In social situations I am someone who always (for example, *says the wrong thing*) _____

_____.

In social situations I am someone who can't (for example, *do small talk*) _____

_____.

In social situations my best attribute is (for example, *being the listener*) _____

_____.

In social situations my worst attribute is (for example, *being the listener*) _____

_____.

Record any other stories your mind generates: _____

_____.

Now that we have covered the most common types of anxious thinking, please return to exercise 6.1, "Your Anxious Thoughts" and, in the "Types of Anxious Thinking" column, fill in as many types of thinking as you can identify for each of the anxious thoughts you recorded. See if you notice any trends. Does your mind tend to use the same type of thinking over and over, or does it prefer variety?

Next, with this information in hand about the types of anxious thinking your mind engages in on your social-anxiety playing field, it's time to explore some defusion strategies.

Defusing from Your Social-Anxiety Thoughts

There are dozens of defusion strategies included in ACT textbooks, self-help books, and websites (some listed in appendix B). In this section, we provide details about the strategies we have found to be particularly helpful in defusing from the socially anxious mind. As you read through them, keep in mind that defusion strategies are not intended to belittle or ridicule your thought processes; they are meant to help you get some distance from your thoughts, notice the process of thinking, and liberate yourself from the tyranny of the fused mind.

"I Am Having the Thought That…"

With this strategy (Hayes 2005), you simply acknowledge that the mind is thinking by saying to yourself, *I am having the thought that* _____ . Try it now by reading aloud the following two sentences, noticing any differences in their emotional impact:

I am going to blush.

I am having the thought that I am going to blush.

What did you notice? Some people find the second sentence to be less anxiety provoking or to seem less "real." Try it again with a thought that is relevant for you.

Naming What the Mind Is Doing

Here you name the type of thinking that your mind is engaged in. Some examples are *I am worrying that my hands will shake, I'm engaged in mind reading right now, I'm doing the post-mortem, I'm "shoulding," There's the imposter story,* and so on.

When our client Sam (the lab worker) noticed the following thought at work, *They can all see me shaking like an idiot,* he said quietly to himself, *Ah, yes, there's the spotlight effect.* He found that this enabled him to get out of his mind and refocus on his task. Defused from his unhelpful thought, he was also better able to get in touch with his value of helping students to learn.

Giving Real Names to Your Thoughts

A fun variation on naming the type of thinking is to give actual names to your thoughts (Hampson 2012), perhaps greeting or chatting with them as you would members of a book club you belong to, for example, *Hello, Mind-Reading Randy; Thanks for showing up, "Shoulding" Shirley; Interesting comments, Negative Nelly.*

Ditching the Meaning of Your Thoughts

Given that we tend to get caught up in the meanings of the words that make up our thoughts, several defusion strategies involve highlighting aspects of words other than their meanings, such as how they sound or look. Here are some examples:

Repetition. Try this now: repeat the word "boring" very quickly for thirty to forty-five seconds, paying attention to how the word sounds as you do it (Hayes 2005). What did you notice? Paul commented that after twenty seconds, he could only hear "boing", and the word lost some of its heaviness for him.

Now try this again with a word or phrase that you tend to fuse with in your feared social situations.

Other voices. Try speaking your thoughts in someone else's voice, such as a television personality, politician (dead or alive), or cartoon character (Hayes 2005).

Singing your thoughts. Try singing your thoughts to the tune of a song such as "Happy Birthday" or to your favorite (or least favorite) pop song (Hayes 2005). Try searching for songs that include phrases that are relevant to you ("He's So Shy" by The Pointer Sisters is an example).

Seeing your thoughts. Notice how your thoughts look by printing, writing, or typing them in different fonts and colors (Harris 2009).

Thanking the Mind

The human mind evolved over many thousands of years in ways that have helped our species to stay alive and pass our genes from generation to generation. Thinking about danger has been helpful in responding to disease, starvation, enemy attacks, and natural disasters, to name just a few dangers. So when your mind thinks about the dangers that await you in social situations, it is just doing its job, and it deserves some credit for that, even if it ultimately is not helpful. Hence, a popular defusion strategy is to thank the mind for thoughts (Hayes 2005), for example, *Thank you, mind, for the thought that I'm going to make a fool of myself.*

You can thank your mind for any type of thought it generates, including memories. For a fun variation on thanking the mind for a memory, try singing your memory to the tune of "Thanks for the Memory." (You can search the Internet for this song. You'll probably recognize the tune but not realize that it's from the movie *The Big Broadcast of 1938.*) Rebecca sang it this way: "Thanks for the memory / of high-school romance / my blunder at the dance" (a double-defusion strategy because it combines thanking the mind with singing thoughts).

A final variation is to thank the processes that helped to shape the mind, such as evolution and genetics, for example, *Thanks, evolution, for keeping my thoughts focused on danger* or *Thank you, Gramps, for passing on your "shyness" genes.*

Defusing with Dr. Phil

On his popular television advice show, *Dr. Phil*, American psychologist Phil McGraw is known for asking, "How's that working for you?" when guests describe the ways they have been addressing their myriad problems. In a similar vein, you can ask how specific thoughts are "working for you." Whenever Jake would consider contacting Kristina for a date, his mind was flooded with thoughts of being unlovable, which caused him to avoid following through with a call or e-mail. When he asked himself, *How are these thoughts working for me?* he was met with a resounding *Not a damned bit!* That allowed him enough space to realize that his fused mind was directing him away from his value of being in a loving relationship. After a few sessions with *Dr. Phil*, he asked Kristina out for coffee.

Developing Awareness of Thinking

At times, we lack awareness of the thoughts that regulate our behavior. Samantha told us, "I'm not sure why I don't speak up in meetings; I just don't." Her actions seemed automatic to her, not influenced by any particular thoughts. As pointed out by Kelly Wilson and Troy Dufrene (2010), just as a troublesome noise in your car can't be fixed if the mechanic can't hear it, you can't defuse from unhelpful thoughts that you aren't aware of. They suggest that sometimes, just "sitting with" a situation can be helpful for identifying fused thoughts. We asked Samantha to sit quietly for a few minutes and notice any thoughts that arose while she imagined a typical work meeting. She was able to get in touch with fearful thoughts of not being able to articulate her ideas to her coworkers. Thought after thought appeared in her mind about being incompetent and not fitting in. She found it helpful to notice them as thoughts, and she also decided to do additional defusion work later, with the particularly troublesome thought *Nobody will respect me if I can't express myself.*

Try "sitting with" the image of one of your feared social situations, with the assistance of the following exercise.

 **Exercise 6.2   Awareness of Thinking**

The purpose of this exercise is to practice awareness of the process of thinking, to watch your mind generating thoughts without getting caught up in the contents of those thoughts. Start by settling into a comfortable sitting position as you bring your attention to the breath, following it as it enters and leaves the body, coming and going of its own accord, allowing the breath to find its own rhythm, not needing to control it in any way.

If you would like to work with a specific social situation, bring it to mind now, getting a clear picture of where you are, who you are with, and what you are doing.

Whenever you are ready, gently shift your awareness to thinking—to paying attention to thoughts as events in the mind. As best you can, bring your awareness to thoughts as they arise in the mind, passing through the space of the mind, and eventually disappearing. There is no need to censor or encourage thinking in any direction, simply allowing thoughts to arise naturally, not holding on to thoughts, pushing them away, or analyzing their contents, simply observing thoughts as events in the field of awareness.

It may help to imagine that you are sitting in a movie theater in front of a large blank screen. As thoughts, memories, and mental images appear in your mind, seeing them projected onto the screen, watching each thought for as long as it remains on the screen.

Thoughts may move slowly or quickly across the screen, some dominating the screen more than others. At times, the screen may go blank; at other times it may be completely filled with thoughts. Whatever is on the screen, remaining curious about the process of thinking itself, noticing your ability to be an impartial observer.

At times you may lose touch with your awareness of thinking, fusing with your thoughts, getting caught up in one of the stories unfolding on the screen. When that happens, returning to the feeling of the breath, not as a way to get away from thoughts or make the mind blank, but as a way to anchor yourself in the present moment, as you escort your mind back to its seat, returning to watching your thoughts coming and going.

What was your experience of that exercise? Did you uncover thoughts that were lurking beneath your awareness, possibly steering you away from your values? If so, you may find it helpful to continue to simply watch those thoughts on your own, or by repeating the "Awareness of Thinking" exercise (using the Mindfulness Log from chapter 4 to record your observations), or you may choose to do further defusion work with them. Doing the "Awareness of Thinking" exercise without any particular situation in mind is also a great way to practice watching thoughts in general.

Observing Your Thoughts

You have already practiced observing your thoughts from your mountain and other observer perspectives (and in the previous exercise). Here are a few more ideas for thought watching.

Thoughts as waterfall metaphor. Imagine that you are standing under a strong waterfall (Segal, Williams, and Teasdale 2002). The water is beating down on your hair and skin, and soaking your clothing. The force of the water is pushing you down. You are so completely immersed in the falling water that you almost feel as if you were a part of it. Now imagine stepping out of the waterfall and standing beside it. You can see the water cascading down and can perhaps feel a fine mist on your skin. You can also see that you are separate from the water; you are not the water. Practice stepping out from the waterfall of your thoughts and watching them, instead of being pushed around and dragged down by them.

Leaves on a stream. Imagine that you are standing beside a stream that has a large maple tree at the edge (Hayes 2005). It's a glorious fall day and the leaves are gradually dropping into the stream. Each leaf has one of your thoughts written on it. Practice watching as each leaf (thought) drops into the water and floats downstream. The stream may flow slowly, quickly, or even come to a complete stop at times. Your task is to simply watch whatever happens. You can also do this exercise online at www.thinkmindfully.com/try-it.

Clouds in the sky. This is similar to the previous metaphor except that your thoughts are written on passing clouds.

Create Your Own Defusion Strategy

Once you have tried the previous defusion strategies, you may want to try your hand at creating your own, something that speaks more directly to you (and it's fun!). Lauren used two old puppets that she had enjoyed playing with as a child to help defuse from anxious thoughts about her upcoming wedding. As one puppet spoke out her fearful thoughts about tripping down the aisle, forgetting her vows, and messing up her speech, the other countered with thoughts about how to avoid these mishaps: *Wear the flat shoes you detest, Keep your vows and speech as short as possible, Cancel the wedding!* As Lauren listened to the drama unfold, she saw that she had the option of not getting caught up in it; instead, she chose to keep her plan to wear "killer" high heels, write meaningful vows, and give a heartfelt speech.

There are infinite possibilities for creating your own personal defusion strategies, as long as each strategy allows you to notice your thoughts as thoughts and not get caught up in their literal meaning. Write down your ideas here: _____

_____

_____

Over the next several weeks, try out all of the defusion strategies (summarized in the box), noting your experiences on the following "Defusing from Your Anxious Thoughts" worksheet (available to download at www.newharbinger.com/20801; make several copies of it or write in a notebook). To get as much practice as possible, try defusing from everyday thoughts (for example, *I am having the thought that I want to eat a muffin for breakfast*) as well as social-anxiety thoughts. You can try some of the strategies right when you notice the thought (for example, naming what the mind is doing or thanking the mind); for others, you may want to wait until you have some time to yourself (for example, ditching the meaning of your thoughts or awareness of thinking). In the latter cases, be sure to jot down the thoughts in a notebook for later use. As you sample the strategies, keep track of the ones that you find most helpful on your social-anxiety playing field. We have found that our clients vary tremendously concerning which strategies they like and find useful. Clearly, "no single size fits all".

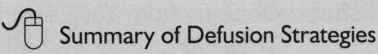 Summary of Defusion Strategies

I am having the thought that: For example, *I am having the thought that I'm making a fool of myself.*

Name what the mind is doing: Name the type of anxious thinking (fortune-telling, mind reading, "shoulding," postmortem, spotlight effect, storytelling, and more basic types, such as worrying and judging).

Give real names to your thoughts: For example, *Mind-Reading Randy.*

Ditch the meanings of your thoughts: Use repetition or other voices, sing them, see them.

Thank the mind: For example, *Thanks for the memory.*

Defuse with Dr. Phil: *How's that thought working for you?*

Awareness of thinking: Listen to the audio download (at www.newharbinger .com/20801) or sit silently with your thoughts.

Observe your thoughts: Use the waterfall metaphor, leaves on a stream, or clouds in the sky.

Create your own defusion strategy:

_____

_____

_____

_____

Finally, this new way of relating to thoughts may take a while to get the hang of, so we recommend practice, practice, and more practice!

Worksheet: Defusing from Your Anxious Thoughts

Thought	Defusion strategy	What did you notice?
Example: *I'm boring.*	Example: *I am having the thought that I'm boring.*	Example: *I had the thought and still contributed to a conversation.*

Your Journey So Far

You have now learned all of the basic skills of the mindfulness and acceptance approach to social anxiety and shyness, thus completing the first leg of your journey through this book. Let's take a moment now to recap what you have learned (and accomplished) so far.

First, you learned about safety mode. You saw that pursuing safety can take you down a dark path—a path of struggle and avoidance—that leads to a restricted life. You also learned that vital-action mode can take you down a different path, the path of a vital and meaningful life. To get going on that path, you started a conversation about what really matters in your life. Next, you learned how paying mindful attention can transform your experience of just about everything: noticing gorillas, eating raisins, viewing nature, and listening to everyday sounds. You learned that remaining present to your direct experience can allow you to see situations more clearly, perhaps even enjoy them more. Building on your mindfulness skills, you then explored a three-pronged approach to strengthening your "abs," to bringing acceptance and compassion to your bodily sensations. Finally, you learned an array of defusion strategies for helping you to "get out of your mind and into your life" (Hayes 2005)!

The Journey Ahead

So far, you have practiced most of your new skills in the relative safety of your home or in other locations outside of your feared ones. It has been kind of like the dress rehearsal before a play, where the actors get onstage and go through their parts without an audience present. In part 2 of this book, you will "have the audience there," so to speak, as you enter your social-anxiety playing field. There, with your new skills in hand, you will finally be ready to operate in vital-action mode: to do what really matters in social situations, as you take your anxious feelings and thoughts along for the ride.

In chapter 7, we introduce you to "VITAL" action and outline a four-part plan for stepping toward your goals. In the final chapter of this book, we continue with "goal stepping," and finish with a "loving-kindness" meditation.

Time to Pause

This might be a good time in your journey through this book to pause, to take some time to practice defusion and other mindfulness skills. If you have been meaning to revise your "Values and Goals Worksheet" (exercise 3.2), now would be a good time, because you will be using it in the next two chapters. On the other hand, you may prefer to continue reading the book at this point. Whenever you decide to move forward to part 2, we'll be here, ready to guide you along your way.

PART 2

Putting It All Together

CHAPTER 7

Taking "VITAL" Action

As we mentioned at the end of the previous chapter, the dress rehearsal is now over! You have practiced your new skills, and now it is time to put them all together and step onto your social-anxiety playing field. That probably sounds pretty scary, so we want to reassure you: you won't be expected to charge onto your field (unless you want to)! Whether you take baby steps or giant leaps, it will be up to you to set your pace. However, you *will* be expected (because you now have the necessary skills) to operate in vital-action mode in your feared social situations.

In this chapter, we introduce "VITAL" action, provide an exercise for walking through it in your imagination, and outline a four-part plan for taking "VITAL" action toward your valued goals.

Introducing "VITAL" Action

You may recall from chapter 2 that the goal in vital-action mode is to live a vital life. The word "vital" is from the Latin word *vitalis*, meaning "of life." Vital-action mode is all about *your* life—about taking action geared toward what really matters to you. The word "VITAL" (in capital letters) will also serve as an acronym as we proceed, a handy way for you to remember to use your new skills: "V" will prompt you to base your actions on your *values and goals*; "I" is to remind you to remain *in the present moment*; "T" is for *taking notice* of your feelings, thoughts, and urges (from your observer perspective); and "AL" is for *allowing* your experience to be exactly as it is. You can print out the following detailed summary of "VITAL Action" to refer to when needed (available for download at www.newharbinger.com/20801).

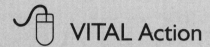

VITAL Action

As you take action on your social-anxiety playing field, you can use the following skills to guide you in each and every action:

V   Identify your *values and goals*. (Hint: Values guide your actions and are never "finished"; goals are things you can check off and say you're done with.)

I   Remain *in the present moment*, first anchoring your attention to the breath and then shifting your focus to, and staying fully present with, what really matters in the situation; revisit your anchor as needed when your focus drifts from the present moment.

T   *Take notice of* your experience from your observer perspective (perhaps embodying your inner mountain or another observer image), noticing feelings, thoughts, and urges to use safety behaviors (including avoidance).

AL *Allow* your experience to be exactly as it is, with the assistance of metaphors (flip on your willingness switch, drop the rope, welcome Uncle Leo, and so on) and defusion strategies (labeling, thank your mind, and so on). Try bringing attitudes of curiosity, openness, compassion, and acceptance to your experience.

Now, to give you a sense of what to expect when you step onto your field, we invite you to try out VITAL action by walking through it first in your imagination. For the following "Imagining VITAL Action" exercise, you have the option of using the written instructions or listening to the corresponding audio (see audio downloads at www.newharbinger. com/20801). First, choose an action or actions to work with during the exercise: perhaps making eye contact, having a short conversation, asking a question, or walking in public—something relevant to one of your goals (from your Values and Goals Worksheet, exercise 3.2). Once you have the situation in mind, proceed to the exercise.

Exercise 7.1   Imagining VITAL Action

This exercise is meant to provide you with an opportunity to practice taking VITAL action in your imagination.

Start by getting into a comfortable position, in a chair or lying down, and allowing your eyes to close gently.

Now bring to mind a situation where you want to take action. Imagine where you are and who you are with, including as many details of the situation as necessary to bring it to life in your mind's eye.

Next, beginning with the "V" in VITAL, representing your "values and goals," get in touch with the value or values that will guide those actions. Why do the actions matter to you? Why are they important? Also, what do you want to accomplish with your actions? Where will they take you? What is your goal?

Now, moving to the "I" in VITAL, "in the present moment," take a few moments to connect with your breathing, coming into the present moment as you pay attention to each complete in-breath, and each complete out-breath, noticing the rising and falling of the breath in your chest and belly. There is no need to control your breathing in any way—simply letting the breath breathe itself, and doing this for several moments, until you are fully present with your breathing. Throughout the remainder of this exercise, whenever your mind wanders from the task at hand, try revisiting the breath as a way of reconnecting with the present moment, and with the exercise.

Now, imagine yourself taking action as you remain focused on your valued goals. And, as you do this, shifting to the final three letters of VITAL, "T," for taking notice of your experience, and "A-L," allowing it to be exactly as it is.

First, noticing any feelings that arise, perhaps observing them from your inner mountain, using another image, or simply watching them. Has fear shown up? Has tension arrived?

Has your heart quickened, or is it hard to catch your breath? Whichever feelings appear, simply observing them with acceptance and compassion, not struggling with them.

Next, noticing thoughts arising about the situation, perhaps worries, evaluations, or mind reading—whatever they are, simply watching your thoughts coming and going. There is no need to think of something else, make the thoughts go away, or resolve anything. Can you thank your mind for anxious thoughts, or defuse from them in another way?

Finally, observing any urges to use safety behaviors, such as hiding your feelings or escaping from the situation. Simply acknowledging any urges and letting go of the need to act on them.

And now, can you make room for the entirety of your experience? Is it something you *must* struggle with, or can you invite it in, saying to yourself with willingness, *Let me feel what there is to be felt because it is my experience right now?*

And, as you gently open up to your experience, watching yourself continue to take action in your imagined situation, focused on what really matters. And doing this for a bit longer.

And when you are ready, letting go of the imagined situation with its accompanying feelings, thoughts, and urges, and directing your focus back to your breath.

Then, gradually widening your attention to take in the sounds in the room. And taking a moment to make the intention to bring this sense of gentle allowing and self-acceptance into the present moment. And when you are ready, slowly opening your eyes.

What was your experience of that exercise? In our work with clients, we have found more variation in their experiences with that exercise than with any other. Our three main observations are as follows:

- Some people are natural "visualizers": they can see a situation unfold in the "mind's eye" as if they were watching a movie. Other people are better at "hearing" a situation: listening to the mind talk about it (silently). Whatever method you use to bring your situation to mind is fine, as long as it helps you to get in touch with your feelings and thoughts about the situation.

- Even when people are able to vividly imagine their situations, there is still considerable variability in their experiences of those situations: some people experience the very same feelings and thoughts they would in their actual situations; some experience different, or muted, feelings and thoughts; and others do not experience any feelings or thoughts about their situations at all.

- Peoples' experiences also vary depending on the situations that are brought to mind. Typically, our clients' top three feared situations tend to evoke more-intense experiences than situations that they fear less.

Given all of this variability, we suggest that you try the exercise with a number of your feared situations in the next few weeks, recording your observations in your "Mindfulness Log" (see chapter 4). If you found that this exercise generated intense experiences (for example, a wildly racing heart or very critical thoughts), try taking a gradual approach when you repeat it. Start by imagining a situation that causes you very mild anxiety, and slowly build toward your top three situations (at your own pace, of course).

When you are using the audio (see the audio downloads at www.newharbinger. com/20801), it can be difficult to choose situations once the audio has started, so make an effort to select a situation in advance. Also, some people prefer fewer instructions; they find it helpful to spend more time on some parts of the acronym "VITAL" (for example, *allowing*) and less time on others (for example, *values and goals*), which is difficult to do when listening to the audio. In this case, doing the exercise from memory would be a good idea, focusing on the parts that are helpful to you.

The way that you worked with VITAL action in your imagination is very similar to how you will take VITAL action on your social-anxiety playing field, outlined next.

A Plan for Taking VITAL Action

In this section, we outline a four-part plan for taking VITAL action as you step toward your goals. The plan is meant to help you choose goals, break them into specific steps (actions), schedule the steps into your week, and carry out the steps (using a worksheet to prepare for each step and to debrief from each completed step). Each part of the plan is depicted in the following flow diagram (figure 7.1), along with the name of the corresponding worksheet or schedule. As we walk you through each part of the plan, we will use examples from Camille's and Jack's very first week of "taking VITAL action."

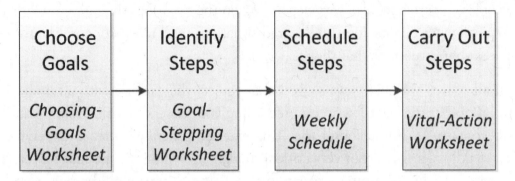

Figure 7.1 A Plan for Taking VITAL Action

Choosing Goals

For this part of the plan, you will need to refer to the "Values and Goals Worksheet" (exercise 3.2) that you completed in chapter 3. (If you didn't complete a worksheet, that's fine; you can do it now.) There are two things involved in choosing goals: identifying life areas to focus on, and choosing specific short-term and long-term goals within those life areas.

Identifying Life Areas

As you recall (and can see if you are looking at your worksheet), the "Values and Goals Worksheet" (exercise 3.2) includes ten different life areas. To start, we recommend that you focus on one to three of the life areas for which you identified values and goals. Which of those areas do you most want to address first? It is important to choose areas that are feasible to work on in the near future. To do this, think about your schedule for the next few months. Are you taking a vacation? Does Thanksgiving (or some other holiday) fall during the next few months? If you will be on vacation, it might be a good time to work on the "leisure" category (if that was an area you had identified as important and relevant). If Thanksgiving falls in the near future, what a great opportunity to work on the "family relationships" life area (and, for comic relief, to watch the very funny movie about family dysfunction at Thanksgiving, *Pieces of April*). It's fine if you choose only one area to focus on. Some of our clients prefer to concentrate their efforts on one life domain for weeks and months at a time.

Short-Term Goals and Long-Term Goals

Some of the goals on your "Values and Goals Worksheet" may be short term, ones that can be accomplished within twelve months (for example, spend more time with friends). Other goals may be long term, ones that will likely take a year or longer to achieve (for example, get married, find a new job). We suggest that you choose one long-term goal and two or three short-term goals that would be feasible for you to start working toward in the near future. In reviewing the goals that you identified in chapter 3, you may decide that none of them is appropriate to start working toward soon. That is fine. Take your time to identify other goals. (Sometimes goals that can be accomplished in fewer than twelve months are broken into three separate categories: immediate, for goals that can be accomplished right away; short term, for goals that can be accomplished within three months; and medium term, for goals that will take from three to twelve months to accomplish. You can use these categories if you prefer.)

Before filling in your "Choosing-Goals Worksheet" (available for download at www.newharbinger.com/20801), first look at Camille's and Jack's worksheets.

Camille's Choosing-Goals Worksheet

Goal	Short- or Long-Term	Life Area
Find a new job.	long-term	career
Talk to one person (friend, acquaintance, coworker) at least once a day.	short-term	social relationships
Work out on the treadmill at the gym.	short-term	health/physical well-being

Jack's Choosing-Goals Worksheet

Goal	Short- or Long-Term	Life Area
Participate in meetings at work.	short-term	career
Give presentation at the annual general meeting.	long-term	career
Ask boss for a raise.	short-term	career

Now, it's time for you to choose three or four goals to start working toward in the coming months. (Additional goals can be added to the "Choosing-Goals Worksheet" later; hence, it has more space than you need for now).

Choosing-Goals Worksheet

Goal	Short- or Long-Term	Life Area

Once you have chosen your goals, the second part of the plan for taking VITAL action involves identifying steps: breaking your goals into specific actions.

Identifying Steps (Specific Actions)

Imagine that your goal is to run a marathon, but you have never run farther than a couple of city blocks. You would likely break your goal into smaller steps, starting with short runs and gradually increasing the duration of each run. In the same vein, perhaps one of your goals is to invite a neighbor to your home for coffee, but you have never exchanged a word with any of your neighbors. You could break that goal into smaller, more specific steps (actions), starting with making eye contact with one neighbor, followed by exchanging a few words with another, and so on, and gradually building toward your goal of inviting a neighbor over for coffee. The number of steps you choose will depend on the pace you set for yourself (a slow pace will require more steps than a fast pace) and how far you are from the goal (the closer you are to the goal, the fewer steps you will need).

We invite you to try out this part of the plan by completing a "Goal-Stepping Worksheet" (available for download at www.newharbinger.com/20801) for one of the goals you identified in the previous section. When breaking goals into specific actions, it is important, whenever possible, to include specific details for each action: where, for how long, and with whom will you carry out a specific action. ("When" is covered in the next part of the plan.) Have a look at the "Goal-Stepping Worksheets" that Camille completed for three of her goals, one for a long-term goal and two for short-term goals.

Camille's Goal-Stepping Worksheet for a Long-Term Goal

My goal is: *to find a new job.*
Step 1: *Attend workshop on résumé writing held at my local employment center.*
Step 2: *Update résumé and show it to my parents for feedback.*
Step 3: *Show résumé to Maggie and Bill for feedback.*
Step 4: *Send résumé to four potential employers.*
Step 5: *Call Aunt Sylvia and Cousin Charlie, and share that my goal is to find a new job.*
Step 6: *Call former colleagues (Jennifer and Dave) to "network."*
Step 7: *Call two potential employers about getting an interview.*
Step 8: *Practice interview in front of the mirror.*
Step 9: *Practice interview with my parents.*
Step 10: *Attend interview.*

Note that Camille was fairly specific about "where" and "with whom" she would carry out her steps.

Camille's Goal-Stepping Worksheet for Short-Term Goal 1

My goal is: *to talk to one person at least once a day.*
Step 1: *Make comment to next-door neighbor about the weather.*
Step 2: *Ask clerk at grocery store how her day is going.*
Step 3: *Ask receptionist at the gym about spinning classes.*
Step 4: *Initiate conversation with Maggie at coffee break (five minutes).*
Step 5: *Chat with coworker in the lunchroom (ten minutes).*
Step 6: *Call Andrea after work (talk for fifteen minutes).*

The next worksheet is for Camille's goal of working out on the treadmill at the gym. You may recall her fear of sweating (from chapter 3). She had avoided using the treadmill because of her concern that she would work up a sweat and people would judge her as "pathetic." Here is her strategy for gradually stepping toward a good workout on the treadmill (sweat and all!).

Camille's Goal-Stepping Worksheet for Short-Term Goal 2

My goal is: *to work out on the treadmill at the gym.*
Step 1: *Walk at a moderate pace for five minutes on the treadmill.*
Step 2: *Walk at a moderate pace for fifteen minutes on the treadmill.*
Step 3: *Run at a moderate pace for five minutes on the treadmill.*
Step 4: *Run at a moderate pace for fifteen minutes on the treadmill.*
Step 5: *Run at a fast pace for five minutes on the treadmill.*
Step 6: *Run at a fast pace for fifteen minutes on the treadmill.*

Note that Camille specified "for how long" she would do each action. Now it's your turn to break one of your goals into steps (you will have an opportunity later in the book to break down the remainder of your goals). There is room for ten steps on the "Goal-Stepping Worksheet" (available for download at www.newharbinger.com/20801 as you need); however, depending on the goal, you may need fewer or more than ten steps.

Goal-Stepping Worksheet

My goal is: _____ .
Step 1:
Step 2:
Step 3:
Step 4:
Step 5:
Step 6:
Step 7:
Step 8:
Step 9:
Step 10:

Scheduling Your Steps

The third part of the goal-stepping plan is to organize the steps from your "Goal-Stepping Worksheets" into a weekly schedule. This part is especially important to help you stay organized when you are using more than one worksheet. Check out Camille's schedule for her first week of goal stepping.

Camille's Weekly Schedule

Sunday	*At the gym: Ask receptionist about the schedule for spinning classes.* *At the gym: Walk at a moderate pace for five minutes on the treadmill.* *Comment to next-door neighbor about the weather.*
Monday	*Talk to Maggie at coffee break (five minutes).* *Attend workshop on résumé writing held at my local employment center.*
Tuesday	*Call Andrea after work (talk for fifteen minutes).* *Update résumé and show it to parents for feedback.*
Wednesday	*Ask cashier at grocery store how her day is going.* *At the gym: Walk at a moderate pace for fifteen minutes on the treadmill.*
Thursday	*Lunch in the staff room: Initiate discussion of upcoming municipal election (ten minutes).* *Show résumé to Maggie for feedback.*
Friday	*Lunch in the staff room (thirty minutes): Start two conversations.*
Saturday	*Call Cousin Charlie and share that my goal is to find a new job.*

Camille managed to fit at least one step into each day of the week and chose to "save" some of them for another week (see her revised "Goal-Stepping Worksheet" in the next chapter). You can use the following "Weekly Schedule" (available for download from www. newharbinger.com/20801) to organize your week-to-week "goal-stepping" when you have finished the next chapter.

Weekly Schedule

Sunday	
Monday	
Tuesday	
Wednesday	
Thursday	
Friday	
Saturday	

If you are starting to think that there is too much "paperwork" involved in this plan, rest assured that we are confident the worksheets will be of benefit to you. Our experience with clients and group members tells us that the "paperwork" provides a structure that will help you to stay on track in stepping toward your goals. Later, once you get the hang of everything, you can start to use your agenda book or phone to schedule your steps for the week.

Once you have a schedule in place for a particular week, the final part of the goal-stepping plan is to carry out each step (and yes, there is more paperwork!).

Carrying Out Your Steps

We have created the "VITAL-Action Worksheet" (available for download at www .newharbinger.com/20801) to help you prepare for and debrief from each of the steps in your weekly schedule. Let's walk through the worksheet next using one of Camille's steps, "Talk to Maggie for five minutes at coffee break," as an example (see her completed worksheet that follows).

1. Preparing for VITAL Action

V: This section of the worksheet is for recording the values and goals that will guide your action. Camille identified "Connecting with others" and "Collegiality" as her values. The corresponding goal that her step was part of (located on one of her "Goal-Stepping Worksheets") was "Talk to one person at least once a day."

I: Here, you can record strategies for remaining "in the present moment." Camille indicated that she would "stay focused on the conversation" and "connect with Maggie's eyes."

T&AL: Here, make note of the anxious feelings, thoughts, and urges to use safety behaviors that you are likely to "take notice of" from your observer perspective during the action (you can also note the "observer image" you plan to use). Depending on what those anticipated experiences are, you can plan for metaphors, defusion strategies, or both to use in the situation; try coming up with brief phrases to encapsulate them (for example, drop the rope, let go, welcome anxiety, thank you mind, and so on). Camille anticipated and planned to welcome sweating; as for thoughts about having nothing interesting to say, she planned to thank her mind for those thoughts if they showed up, and let go of the familiar urge to ask too many questions (as a way to avoid the discomfort of talking about herself).

Other Preparation: Here, you can record anything else that could be helpful. For example, if you anticipate intense physical sensations, you could practice accepting that type of sensation in advance by going through the "Being with Your Anxiety" exercise from chapter 5 (exercise 5.3), just as Camille planned to practice acceptance of sweating. Specific mindfulness exercises, such as the "Body Scan" (exercise 5.1), done on your own or using the audio (see the audio downloads at www.newharbinger.com/20801), could also be useful if you anticipate intense bodily sensations. Other suggestions are to do the "Imagining VITAL Action" exercise (exercise 7.1) the night before (or morning of) your chosen action, or to review the "VITAL" acronym in your mind before starting the step, perhaps just before you leave home, as you ride the bus to work, or just before joining a social gathering or giving a presentation.

2. Debriefing VITAL Action

The "Debriefing VITAL Action" section of the worksheet is for recording what happened when you carried out the step, including successes and barriers, and for noting things you can do to address those barriers in the future. Your willingness switch is bound to slip off when carrying out some of your steps, even when you have carefully prepared. Whenever that happens, note what you are struggling with: if you tend to fuse with anxious thoughts as you take vital action, you can always review defusion strategies; if you tend to struggle with anxious feelings, you may want to revisit the "abs" exercises in chapter 5. You can also consider how best to change the details of the specific steps you intend to repeat.

Camille forgot to thank her mind for unhelpful thoughts, and instead gave in to its "advice" to cut the conversation short. To address this, she planned to repeat the action, reviewing the acronym "VITAL" in her mind before going to the break room and reducing the duration of talking from five to two minutes (and she revised her weekly schedule accordingly).

Camille's VITAL-Action Worksheet

My Action/Step: *Talk with Maggie for five minutes at coffee break.*

1. Preparing for VITAL Action

V: What are the values and goals underlying the action?

Values: <u>*Connecting with others, collegiality.*</u>   Goals: <u>*Talk to one person at least once a day.*</u>

I: How will you remain in the present moment during the action?

<u>*stay focused on the conversation; connect with Maggie's eyes*</u>

T: What internal experiences are you likely to take notice of during the action (using which observer image)? *and*

AL: What strategies can you use to allow your experience to be while taking action?

observer image: <u>*I'll watch from my inner mountain.*</u>

feelings: <u>*Sweating is sure to show up; welcome it.*</u>

thoughts: <u>*I have nothing interesting to say; thank my mind for unhelpful thoughts.*</u>

urges to use safety behaviors: <u>*Watch out for the urge to ask too many questions in order to control my discomfort about talking about myself; welcome and let go of urges instead of acting on them.*</u>

other preparation: <u>*Practice acceptance of sweating exercise the night before.*</u>

2. Debriefing VITAL Action

What happened, including successes and barriers: <u>*I managed to talk to Maggie and be fully present for a whole minute, by staying connected with the conversation and her eyes. Then I forgot to thank my mind for unhelpful thoughts; I followed its stupid advice to cut the conversation short (because I was clearly boring Maggie, or so my mind told me).*</u>

Actions to address barriers, if applicable: <u>*I'll review the "VITAL" acronym in my mind before going to the break room next time. I'll try for a two-minute conversation instead of five minutes.*</u>

At this time, we invite you to try out the worksheet, and "take VITAL action", for one specific step, right now. If feasible, you could revisit the situation you used earlier in the chapter for the "Imagining VITAL Action exercise", you could choose one of the steps from the "Goal-Stepping Worksheet" you completed earlier, or you could identify another action that would be feasible to carry out right now (perhaps make a phone call, have a conversation with someone close by, and so on). Start by completing the "Preparing for VITAL Action" section of the "VITAL-Action Worksheet" (available for download at www.new harbinger.com/20801). Fill in the "Debriefing VITAL Action" section after you have taken action.

VITAL-Action Worksheet

My Action/Step: _____

1. Preparing for VITAL Action

V: What are the values and goals underlying the action?

Value(s):_____Goal(s):_____

I: How will you remain in the present moment during the action?

_____

T: What internal experiences are you likely to take notice of during the action (using which observer image)? *and*

AL: What strategies can you use to allow your experience to be while taking action?

observer image: _____

feelings: _____

_____

thoughts: _____

_____

urges to use safety behaviors: _____

_____

Other preparation: _____

2. Debriefing VITAL Action

What happened, including successes and barriers? _____

_____

Actions to address barriers, if applicable: _____

_____

You have now sampled each part of the basic plan for "taking VITAL action" on your social-anxiety playing field. We presented a fair bit of material so you may find it helpful at this point to review part, or all, of chapter 7 (You can also come back to it at any time).

In the final chapter of this book, we suggest ways to maximize your goal-stepping experience as you step toward your vital life!

CHAPTER 8

Stepping Toward
Your Vital Life

In the previous chapter, you took an initial foray into a four-part plan for taking action toward your goals. In this chapter we build on that plan with suggestions for getting the most out of "goal stepping," as you move forward in the weeks and months ahead. We finish with an exercise about bringing compassion to yourself and others.

Getting the Most Out of Goal Stepping

In this section we outline a number of things you can do to maximize your success at goal stepping. First, we look at enlisting other people to help you.

Enlisting the Help of Others (Role-Playing)

In our therapy groups, we typically practice taking vital action with the help of role-playing, where group members take turns working on specific goals with the assistance of other group members. For example, if one group member wants to practice being interviewed for a job, another group member will volunteer to play the role of the interviewer. With a little creativity, we are able to come up with role-plays to address many different types of goals.

Fortunately, you don't need to attend a therapy group to benefit from role-playing. You can ask friends, family members, and coworkers to help you. If you are seeing a therapist one-on-one, your therapist may be willing to participate in role-plays. Role-playing is particularly suited for situations that don't occur on a regular basis (where there is little opportunity to practice in the "actual" situations). Typical situations of this type are getting married, attending job interviews, and public speaking. If you have goals related to these types of situations, it can be very helpful to include role-plays in your "Goal-Stepping Worksheets," just as Camille included a "practice" job interview with her parents in her worksheet related to getting a job.

One of the benefits of role-playing is that you can instruct your "helper" to act in certain ways. In the case of a job interview, you could ask your helper to role-play an interviewer who is friendly, is encouraging, asks easy questions, asks difficult questions, is rude, is critical, is dismissive of you, or whichever "interviewer style" you would like to practice being willing to experience. In addition to job interviews, you can also "set up" specific details for role-plays of other situations, such as directing your helper to disagree with you about an issue, to compliment or criticize you about your appearance, to ask increasingly personal questions, to make unreasonable requests, and so on (see the section "Intentionally Bringing on Your Feared Outcomes," later in this chapter). The bottom line is that role-playing is suitable for *any* situation if it can help you to step toward your goals.

It is best to recruit "helpers" who you anticipate will be patient and supportive. You will need to say something about why you are asking for their help; however, you can choose to share as little or as much as you want about your struggles with social anxiety, depending on your goals. If one of your goals is to share more about yourself with others, then sharing information about your social fears with your intended helpers could be a step toward that goal. If sharing is not one of your goals, you could simply approach them for help "with a situation that you are nervous about" (most people are nervous about job interviews and giving speeches).

Goal-Stepping for Specific Social Situations

There is no reason to "reinvent the wheel" when you are breaking down your goals into specific steps. If you found it difficult in the previous chapter to come up with ideas for specific steps to use in certain social situations, you may find it helpful to see what has "worked" for others. In this section we offer suggestions for actions to try out in specific social situations (many of which our clients have found helpful in stepping toward their goals). The section is divided into the three types of social situations that were outlined in the first chapter, starting with situations involving social interaction.

Situations Involving Social Interaction

Situations involving social interaction are about communicating with other people (in person, talking on the phone, "texting," e-mailing, and so on), and can be further divided into a number of different subcategories.

Casual conversations. If one of your goals is to increase your engagement in casual conversations, there are a number of "tried and true" steps for gradually approaching that goal. You could start by saying "hi" to people you encounter, such as cashiers, waiters, and receptionists. As a next step, you could exchange a few words with people in lines, on elevators, in waiting rooms, at bus stops, and at sporting or cultural events. As your willingness switch gets stronger, you can gradually engage in longer and longer conversations with people. Other options include talking with dog owners or parents as you watch your dogs or children at play, and taking advantage of each and every opportunity to chat with friends, neighbors, family members, coworkers, and fellow students. This may require changing old habits (safety behaviors) of arriving late to class, declining invitations from friends, or avoiding the staff room and family events. For example, if you have been avoiding spending time in your front yard, you may choose to spend some time gardening, watching your children at play, or sitting on the porch, taking advantage of opportunities to say hello to neighbors and passersby.

Online communication. Communicating online can be a goal in and of itself, or it can serve as a step toward in-person communication. Sending an e-mail can be a first step in the direction of reconnecting with someone. Joining an online group can be a way of connecting with people who have similar interests that may lead to in-person outings. Online dating has become quite popular and can be a very helpful way to start dating. Creating a profile, browsing other peoples' profiles, and sending e-mails to prospective dates can be initial steps.

Speaking on the telephone. You can make inquiries by phone at different types of businesses (for example, stores and service companies) or government offices, initiate calls to old friends or family members you haven't spoken to in a while, or increase the duration of calls to those you typically speak with. Try answering the phone every time it rings if you have been avoiding that, even if it means engaging in conversation with telemarketers!

Sending back and returning items. Are you nervous about telling servers at restaurants that mistakes have been made with your orders? Try a gradual approach to sending back food, perhaps starting with something like asking for hotter water for your tea. A more advanced step might be to order a food item cooked in a certain way (for example, asking for a steak "rare") and then return it to the server, stating that it has not been cooked properly.

In the same vein, do you have clothing at home that doesn't fit you well, or appliances that don't work properly because you were too nervous to return them? Try a gradual approach to returning items, perhaps starting with inexpensive items (to "friendly stores") and working your way up to more expensive items (to stores that are known to give people a hard time about returning items).

Asking for assistance. Options include asking for the time or for directions from strangers (including police officers), asking questions of teachers or professors after class or during their office hours, asking for assistance from salespeople, asking your friends or family to bring food to a gathering you are hosting, and asking a small favor of a neighbor, such as keeping an eye on your house or watering your plants when you're away.

Expressing opinions. Try introducing and expressing your opinions about various topics during conversations, perhaps about a recent movie, local election, or other news event. As you repeat this practice, you could choose topics with increasingly greater degrees of controversy. In our groups we often debate the controversial local bylaw that bans people from owning pit bulls. Group members find it particularly challenging to argue the side of the debate that they don't actually support; try that approach as an advanced practice!

Being Observed

If you are working on goals in this category, there are many actions that can be easily integrated into your day-to-day activities, depending on your usual schedule. Instead of gravitating to areas that minimize your chances of being observed, try to choose more-crowded locations. Here are some actions that have worked for our clients:

- Walk down the "busy" side of the street, or choose a busier route to walk than the one you usually take.

- Go to your gym at the busiest time and work out in the most crowded area.

- Stand at the front or in the middle of an exercise class, or put your yoga mat in the middle of the yoga studio.

- Dance at a party, rather than sit on the sidelines.

- Ride the bus, streetcar, or subway at rush hour.

- Go shopping when the stores are more likely to be crowded and the lines long, or choose the longest line at the grocery store.

- Ride elevators in busy office buildings, hospitals, or other public buildings.

- Jog in a crowded park.

- Walk around at a street fair, carnival, or other public outdoor activity.

- Eat in a crowded food court or in the lunchroom at work, or purchase messy items to eat at a restaurant.

- Use your phone in a busy public place, such as a mall.

- Ask a coworker to observe you as you work.

- Walk into a lecture theater or classroom from the front rather than the back, or if you have to walk in from the back, take a seat at the front.

- Offer to write something on the board in class.

- Offer to serve drinks or snacks at a gathering.

- Throw a ball around with a child or dog in front of your house or in a park.

Performance Situations

It can be challenging to find opportunities to step toward performance goals if these types of situations are not part of your daily routine. But with a little creativity (and assistance from your "helpers"), you can find a number of different ways to do it. The following ways have been helpful for our clients.

Speaking up in groups. Try asking questions or contributing your views during meetings at work and in the community, such as meetings of a parent-teacher organization, political party, board of a local charity, Rotary Club, book club, or religious group. If you don't belong to such an organization, consider joining one. Consider attending and asking questions at public lectures, often offered at universities, libraries, museums, and community centers.

Giving talks. You can be proactive and offer to give a presentation to colleagues; talk at a local school about your work; offer to give a toast at a wedding, birthday, or retirement party; or say a few words about the deceased at a funeral. It can be helpful to first practice presentations or speeches in front of family or friends.

Many of our clients have joined Toastmasters International (www.toastmasters.org), a nonprofit organization that helps people to develop their public-speaking skills. It is available in 116 countries, so there is likely at least one meeting location near you! You can visit a meeting for free, so perhaps visit several and find the one that suits you best.

Reading aloud. This is a very popular practice in our groups, especially for those who are self-conscious about their speaking skills (in particular, when English is not their first language). You can recruit family and friends to listen to you read aloud, or consider volunteering to read a passage at your place of worship.

Performing arts. Many people find it easier to perform in front of children or the elderly. If you are working on goals related to the performing arts—playing an instrument, singing, acting, or another talent—you could offer to perform at a nursery school, day care center, children's hospital, retirement home, nursing home, and so on. If you are working up to performing in front of a large audience, you could offer to perform in front of small groups of family members or friends, or at "smallish" events such as bridal showers and birthday parties.

Job interviews. As mentioned earlier in this chapter, role-playing can be helpful in preparing for job interviews. You could also apply for jobs that you don't really want just to get practice at interviewing.

Intentionally Bringing on Your Feared Outcomes

People often tell us that they have little opportunity to practice "being with" the things they fear will happen in social situations, because those things rarely happen! Now, sometimes the "feared outcomes" aren't occurring because people are avoiding their feared situations (for example, Mary had never tripped on her wedding dress while walking "down the aisle," because she had avoided getting married). In other cases, the feared outcomes have occurred a few times in the past, but not recently (for example, Bob had felt dizzy a few times as a teenager, when he was talking to attractive girls at parties; well into his twenties, when we met him, it hadn't happened in years; however, he continued to worry about it and would stay seated when talking to attractive women, "just in case"). In other instances, the feared outcomes have *never* occurred, yet people still worry about them (for example, Amy, an actor, feared that her mind would go blank during a performance and she wouldn't be able to continue, even though that had never happened to her).

One approach to practicing "being with" outcomes that rarely (or never) occur is to *intentionally* bring them on, just as you intentionally brought on bodily sensations of anxiety in chapter 5 (exercise 5.3). For that exercise, you practiced in the relative "safety" of your home. You may recall that some people don't find that exercise to be very helpful, because they are only concerned about their anxious symptoms when they are around other people. If that is the case for you, you can take the exercise "up a notch" and intentionally bring on bodily sensations *in* your feared social situations. Bob tried this out by spinning in a chair (after reviewing the "VITAL" acronym) just before his sister's very pretty friend, Miranda, was due to arrive at their house. He greeted Miranda at the door, feeling dizzy *and* standing up! He found that when he focused on his valued goal of finding a girlfriend, he was able to complete the step he had set for himself ("Have a two-minute conversation with Miranda while feeling dizzy").

You can also intentionally bring on other types of feared outcomes. For example, you can intentionally spill a drink at a restaurant, mess up your words during a speech, or say something nonsensical or boring during a conversation. If you fear that you will "annoy" or "inconvenience" people, you can purposely do things that you imagine will bring on those outcomes. For example, you can remain stopped at a traffic light even after the light turns green, take twelve items to the "express" checkout (when the limit is eight items), or slowly dig out change from your purse to pay for your purchase when there is a long line behind you. Role-playing can be very useful for intentionally bringing on feared outcomes, because you can instruct your helper to do the things you fear, such as criticize you, ignore you, or act in an angry manner.

The idea behind this approach is to provide you with opportunities to stay focused on your goals and allow your anxiety to be present even when your worst fears are also "present." This is usually considered an "advanced practice," to be attempted after you have had the chance to strengthen your willingness switch with less-challenging steps.

Social Anxiety and Shyness Support Groups

Some cities have social anxiety and shyness support groups. In addition to being helpful as a form of social support, they can serve as places to carry out some of the steps from your "Goal-Stepping Worksheets" (see chapter 7) (for example, "engage in conversations") and to recruit helpers for steps that involve role-plays. Find out if there is a local support group in your city.

Skill Development

Skill development can be part of your overall plan for stepping toward your goals. You can search the Internet for local courses or workshops on skills such as assertiveness, public speaking, the art of conversation, and dating, to name a few. You can also search for books and other resources on these topics.

Stepping into the Future

In this section, we look at using your VITAL-action plan to move forward into the weeks and months ahead as you step toward your vital future!

Choosing Goals for the Future

In the previous chapter you completed a "Choosing-Goals Worksheet" for a period of time that encompassed the next few months. However, you may prefer to start with a plan that focuses on a shorter or longer period of time. A one-year time frame is a popular starting point for some of our clients, whereas others prefer to create five-year or ten-year plans. No single time frame is right or wrong. Choose a time period that makes sense to you, given your current life circumstances. For example, if there is a lot of uncertainty in your life right now (for example, you're waiting to hear about acceptance to college or a new job, or there is serious illness in your family), it might be best to plan for a shorter period of time until things sort themselves out. Once you have decided on a time frame, revisit your "Choosing-Goals Worksheet" from the previous chapter and consider the following questions: Are there goals you would like to add to your existing list? Are there any you would like to take off the list? Are there additional life areas you would like to focus on? If so, what are your goals for those life domains? Many of our clients like to keep separate lists of goals for different "Life Areas," such as one list for "Career" and another for "Relationships." See what works for you as you proceed now with revising your "Choosing-Goals Worksheet" (or as you create new ones).

Identifying Steps

In the previous chapter you completed a "Goal-Stepping Worksheet" for one of your goals. Now that you have more information about how to get the most out of goal-stepping, we invite you to complete separate worksheets (print off as many copies as you need of the "Goal-Stepping Worksheet" from www.newharbinger.com/20801) for the remaining goals listed on your revised "Choosing-Goals Worksheet" (or worksheets; see above). Remember to be specific about where, with whom, and for how long you will do each action (where relevant). As you make progress toward your goals from week to week, you can revise your worksheets accordingly, crossing off completed steps and adding new ones as necessary. After her first week of goal stepping, Camille revised her worksheet (below) for her long-term goal of finding a job. She deleted the steps she had completed and added several others.

Camille's Revised Goal-Stepping Worksheet for a Long-Term Goal

My goal is: *to find a new job.*
Step 1: *Show résumé to Bill for feedback.*
Step 2: *Send résumé to ten potential employers.*
Step 3: *Call Aunt Sylvia and share that my goal is to find a new job.*
Step 4: *Call former colleagues (Jennifer and Dave) to "network."*
Step 5: *Call two potential employers about getting an interview.*
Step 6: *Practice interview in front of the mirror.*
Step 7: *Practice interview with my parents.*
Step 8: *Attend workshop on interviewing held by my local employment center.*
Step 9: *Attend interviews for jobs I don't want (for practice).*
Step 10: *Attend interview for job I'm really interested in.*

As you get the hang of goal stepping (and you will!), you may find yourself breaking down goals into steps "in your head" (especially for short-term goals), and written worksheets can be gradually phased out. It is best to stick with the worksheets (or another format you may prefer) for long-term goals.

Scheduling Steps

People have different methods of scheduling their steps. The method you use—the "Weekly Schedule" from chapter 7, day planner, notebook, smartphone, and so on—doesn't matter; having a schedule is what counts. Scheduling is an important tool to help you stay on track in stepping toward your goals.

Carrying Out Steps

As outlined in the previous chapter, we recommend that you complete "VITAL-Action Worksheets" to help you to prepare for and debrief from individual steps. Hold off on filling out the "Preparing for VITAL Action" sections of the worksheets until the day before each step is scheduled to be carried out. In that way, you can prepare for a specific day based on your progress on the previous day. You may find that you can reuse the "preparing" sections of worksheets for steps that are similar to each other or for steps that you are repeating. Camille reused the "preparing" part of the worksheet she had completed for the step "Talk to Maggie for five minutes at coffee break." She repeated that step for gradually longer periods, eventually enjoying an hour-long chat with Maggie at lunchtime. She also reused the "preparing" section of that worksheet for other steps relevant to her goal of "talking to one person at least once a day." When you really have the hang of taking VITAL action, you can gradually phase out the worksheets. If you run into problems later, you can always return to the worksheets until you get back on track.

You may also find it useful to keep the "VITAL Action" summary box handy (see chapter 7, and available to download at www.newharbinger.com/20801). You could store it in your smartphone, write it on a card to keep in your wallet or purse, or whatever works best for you.

Roadblocks on Your Path

As you step toward your goals, you will most likely experience roadblocks along the way. You may be faced with illness, a job loss, or other stressors. You may find yourself completely offtrack at times. That is to be expected, especially if the approach outlined in this book is completely new to you. It will take time to strengthen your new skills, and it is important to be patient with yourself throughout the process. Whenever you do find yourself offtrack, use the experience as an opportunity to review your goals and get back in touch with your values, without giving yourself a hard time about it; to be kind and understanding with yourself, rather than judging yourself; and to have self-compassion. That brings us to the final topic.

Bringing Compassion to Yourself and Others

There is growing research evidence for the benefits of self-compassion for many problems, including anxiety (Neff 2012). Of course, compassion is inherent in the attitude of nonjudging and acceptance that you have been cultivating all along in the various mindfulness practices. We want to end with an ancient meditation practice called loving-kindness that addresses compassion more explicitly. In the following exercise, you will be invited to get in touch with an attitude of caring and compassion, direct it to yourself, and then expand it to others.

 **Exercise 8.1   Loving-Kindness**

Start by getting into a comfortable position and allowing your eyes to close gently. Now, take a few moments to get in touch with the physical sensations in your body, especially the sensations of touch or pressure where your body makes contact with the chair or floor. Notice the gentle rising and falling of the breath in your chest and belly. There is no need to control your breathing in any way—simply let the breath breathe itself.

Now, bringing to mind a picture of yourself, in your mind's eye, say quietly to yourself: *May I be safe. May I be free from suffering. May I be at peace.*

Next, bringing to mind someone you care about, a friend, family member, or other loved one, perhaps even a beloved pet. And with your loved one in mind, repeating to yourself: *May he/she be safe. May he/she be free from suffering. May he/she be at peace.*

Now bringing to mind someone who is going through a difficult time; is perhaps ill or struggling with another problem. Expanding the field of loving-kindness to this person by repeating to yourself: *May he/she be safe. May he/she be free from suffering. May he/she be at peace.*

Next, bringing to mind an acquaintance, someone you may know from work, or who lives in your neighborhood, someone you don't know very well and don't have strong feelings about, a neutral person. And offering loving-kindness to this person as you repeat to yourself: *May he/she be safe. May he/she be free from suffering. May he/she be at peace.*

Next, thinking of someone who you don't like, perhaps someone who has wronged you in some way, or a politician or other well-known person who you dislike for other reasons. Trying not to get caught up in the reasons for disliking the person you brought to mind, extending compassion to this person as well: *May he/she be safe. May he/she be free from suffering. May he/she be at peace.*

Now, bringing all of the above people under the umbrella of loving-kindness: yourself, the person you care about, the person who is struggling, the acquaintance, and the person you don't like. *May they be safe. May they be free from suffering. May they be at peace.*

Next, opening up to include everyone in your life, sending compassion and loving-kindness to them: *May they be safe. May they be free from suffering. May they be at peace.*

And finally, extending the field of loving-kindness to include all living beings. Repeating to yourself: *May they be safe. May they be free from suffering. May they be at peace.*

Now, gently letting go of specific thoughts of loving-kindness, bringing your attention back to the breath and to the sense of the body as a whole. And perhaps making the intention to take an attitude of compassion and loving-kindness toward yourself and others, throughout the rest of your day.

And whenever you are ready, gently opening your eyes.

If the repeated phrases in the exercise did not resonate with you, feel free to choose ones that do. Be sure to record your experiences with the loving-kindness meditation in your "Mindfulness Log" (see chapter 4). Some people find it helpful to silently repeat certain phrases as they go about their day-to-day activities. Camille found it helpful to repeat to herself *May I live a vital life* on occasions when she was struggling more than usual with anxious thoughts and feelings. We hope this exercise will help you to be more kind and understanding with yourself (and others) as you continue along this journey.

Closing Comments

We have come to the end of our journey together. It has been an honor to accompany and guide you along the way. We are very excited about the growing body of research evidence that supports the effectiveness of mindfulness and acceptance–based approaches for social anxiety. We have summarized the evidence for you in appendix A. There is also a list of recommended reading and websites that may be of interest to you.

We sincerely hope you have benefited from the book and will continue to benefit as you move toward a life that really matters to you, toward your vital future. We wish you all the best as you continue on your journey.

Mindfulness and Acceptance Approaches for Social Anxiety Disorder—The Evidence

Mindfulness and Acceptance–Based Interventions

Mindfulness and acceptance–based interventions (MABIs) have been used for a variety of problems, with good evidence supporting them. There are several therapies that fall under this umbrella. We focus here on the three that were defined in the introduction, because these are the three that are most relevant to social anxiety:

- Acceptance and commitment therapy (ACT)

- Mindfulness-based cognitive therapy (MBCT)

- Mindfulness-based stress reduction (MBSR)

What these therapies have in common is that they encourage people to take a mindful, accepting stance to thoughts and feelings.

MABIs for Social Anxiety

At this writing, there are nine studies investigating the use of MABIs for social anxiety disorder. These studies were conducted in five countries: Canada, Denmark, The Netherlands, the United States, and Sweden.

Open Trials

The first step in evaluating a new treatment is usually an *open trial*: the new treatment is offered to a group of patients, but is not compared to another treatment or control group. Five of the nine studies were uncontrolled, open trials of that nature:

- Two open trials looked at MBSR and MBCT, one where clients were seen in groups (MBSR) (Goldin, Ramel, and Gross 2009) and another where they were seen one on one (adapted MBCT, with additional elements) (Bögels, Sijbers, and Voncken 2006).

- Two open trials investigated ACT for social anxiety disorder, one where clients were seen in groups (Ossman et al. 2006) and another where they were seen individually (Dalrymple and Herbert 2007).

- The remaining study is our mindfulness and acceptance–based group therapy (MAGT) open trial (Kocovski, Fleming, and Rector 2009), which we say more about later.

All of these open trials showed promising results:

- There were significant improvements in social anxiety in all five studies.

- The improvements were similar in size to what is typically seen in traditional cognitive behavioral therapy (CBT).

- Some studies also measured depression, mindfulness, acceptance, valued living, or some combination, and showed improvements in these other areas as well.

Overall, these open trials provided initial support for the use of MABIs for social anxiety disorder.

Randomized Controlled Trials

The next step is to conduct a randomized controlled trial (RCT) in which the new treatment is compared to one or more "control conditions." The control conditions can include other treatments or no treatment at all. Participants are randomly assigned to conditions; in other words, they agree to be placed in any of the conditions, and the condition they end up in is determined by chance (for example, by a coin toss). Four of the studies were of this nature, all of which compared a MABI to traditional CBT:

- The earliest study (presented at a conference but not yet published in a scientific journal) compared ACT to CBT; both treatments were brief (only four sessions) and had individual and group components (Morén and Wiwe 2006).

- The next two studies were done in groups, and each compared MBSR or MBCT with CBT (MBSR: Koszycki et al. 2007; MBCT: Piet et al. 2010).

- Finally, there is our RCT, which was done in groups and compared MAGT to CBT and a waiting-list control group (Kocovski et al. under review). We say more about our study later.

Here is a summary of the results of the four RCTs:

- Three studies found the MABI and CBT to be equivalent as far as improvements in social anxiety.

- When depression, disability, quality of life, valued living, acceptance, or some combination were measured, most often results continued to be very similar when comparing the different treatments.

- One study found CBT to be more effective than the MABI (Koszycki et al. 2007). The MABI was MBSR delivered by a layperson, and it was not adapted for use with social anxiety, whereas CBT was delivered by an experienced therapist and had about half as many patients in the groups. Even under these circumstances, patients in MBSR improved significantly, but just not as much as the CBT patients.

- One other study also had such issues: fewer participants and about double the therapy hours in the CBT condition compared to the MABI (Piet et al. 2010), but for this study, the MABI and CBT were found to have similar results.

Overall, there is a growing body of evidence that MABIs are effective for social anxiety disorder, and they offer an alternative to traditional CBT.

MAGT for Social Anxiety Disorder

We will give you more detail on the group-therapy approach we developed for social anxiety disorder, given that much of this book follows from this work.

MAGT Open Trial

Our first study was an open trial to determine whether a mindfulness and acceptance–based approach was feasible and helpful for the socially anxious clients at our clinic (Kocovski, Fleming, and Rector 2009). As described in the introduction, MAGT is basically ACT with enhanced mindfulness taken from MBCT and MBSR. We ran five such groups (forty-two people total) and made some changes along the way, based on the feedback we received from the group participants. We found that on average, people became less socially anxious and less depressed, and more mindful and accepting, and tended to dwell on things less than before. These results were similar to what we were finding with the CBT groups in the same clinic. We were motivated to continue on this path.

MAGT Randomized Controlled Trial

Our second study was a randomized controlled trial where people had to agree to be in MAGT or group CBT, or stay on a waiting list for twelve weeks and then receive treatment (Kocovski et al. under review). The study included 137 people total, 53 in each treatment, and 31 on the waiting list. Our main result was that both treatments led people to be less socially anxious, but they weren't different from one another; people in MAGT improved just as much as people in group CBT. We also found that being more mindful and accepting contributed to people being less socially anxious at the end of treatment. We also followed people for three months after their treatment ended, and they were able to maintain the gains they had made with treatment.

APPENDIX B

Additional Resources

Acceptance and Commitment Therapy (ACT)

The following two books provide excellent overviews of ACT (for targeting all problems, including anxiety):

Harris, R. 2008. *The Happiness Trap: How to Stop Struggling and Start Living.* Boston: Trumpeter Books.

Hayes, S. C. 2005. *Get Out of Your Mind and Into Your Life: The New Acceptance and Commitment Therapy.* With S. Smith. Oakland, CA: New Harbinger Publications.

Mindfulness-Based Cognitive Therapy (MBCT)

Segal, Z. V., J. M. G. Williams, and J. D. Teasdale. 2002. *Mindfulness-Based Cognitive Therapy for Depression: A New Approach to Preventing Relapse.* New York: The Guilford Press.

Williams, M., J. Teasdale, Z. Segal, and J. Kabat-Zinn. 2007. *The Mindful Way through Depression: Freeing Yourself from Chronic Unhappiness*. New York: The Guilford Press.

Mindfulness-Based Stress Reduction (MBSR)

Kabat-Zinn, J. 1990. *Full Catastrophe Living: Using the Wisdom of Your Body and Mind to Face Stress, Pain, and Illness*. New York: Dell Publishing.

Stahl, B., and E. Goldstein. 2010. *A Mindfulness-Based Stress Reduction Workbook*. Oakland, CA: New Harbinger Publications.

Mindfulness and Acceptance Approaches to Anxiety

The following three books focus on all types of anxiety (including social anxiety):

Forsyth, J. P., and G. H. Eifert. 2007. *The Mindfulness and Acceptance Workbook for Anxiety: A Guide to Breaking Free from Anxiety, Phobias, and Worry Using Acceptance and Commitment Therapy*. Oakland, CA: New Harbinger Publications.

Orsillo, S. M., and L. Roemer. 2011. *The Mindful Way through Anxiety: Break Free from Chronic Worry and Reclaim Your Life*. New York: The Guilford Press.

Wilson, K. G., and T. Dufrene. 2010. *Things Might Go Terribly, Horribly Wrong: A Guide to Life Liberated from Anxiety*. Oakland, CA: New Harbinger Publications.

Social Anxiety and Shyness

Antony, M. M., and R. P. Swinson. 2008. *The Shyness and Social Anxiety Workbook: Proven, Step-by-Step Techniques for Overcoming Your Fear*. 2nd ed. Oakland, CA: New Harbinger Publications. (This book provides an excellent overview of many aspects of social anxiety and shyness, including causes, cognitive behavioral approaches, and medications.)

Henderson, L. 2011. *The Compassionate-Mind Guide to Building Social Confidence: Using Compassion-Focused Therapy to Overcome Shyness and Social Anxiety.* Oakland, CA: New Harbinger Publications.

Furthering Your Practice of Mindfulness and Acceptance

There is a rapidly growing number of books available on the topics of mindfulness and acceptance. The following books represent some of our favorites.

Brach, T. 2004. *Radical Acceptance: Embracing Your Life with the Heart of a Buddha.* New York: Bantam.

Chödrön, P. 1997. *When Things Fall Apart: Heart Advice for Difficult Times.* Boston: Shambhala Publications.

Kabat-Zinn, J. 1994. *Wherever You Go, There You Are: Mindfulness Meditation in Everyday Life.* New York: Hyperion.

———. 2005. *Coming to Our Senses: Healing Ourselves and the World through Mindfulness.* New York: Hyperion.

Siegel, D. J. 2007. *The Mindful Brain: Reflection and Attunement in the Cultivation of Well-Being.* New York: W.W. Norton and Company.

Thich Nhat Hanh. 1996. *The Miracle of Mindfulness: An Introduction to the Practice of Meditation.* Translated by M. Ho. Boston: Beacon Press.

Internet Resources

Association for Contextual Behavioral Science (ACBS) (contextualscience.org): This site includes helpful information about acceptance and commitment therapy. You can search for an ACT therapist in your geographical area by clicking on "Find an ACT Therapist."

ACT for the Public, Yahoo Groups (health.groups.yahoo.com/group/ACT_for_the_Public/): A public discussion group.

University of Massachusetts Medical School Center for Mindfulness in Medicine, Health Care, and Society (w3.umassmed.edu/MBSR/public/searchmember.aspx). You can search for MBSR programs worldwide.

References

American Psychiatric Association. 2004. *Diagnostic and Statistical Manual of Mental Disorders, Fourth Edition, Text Revision*. Washington, DC: Author.

Antony, M. M., and R. P. Swinson. 2008. *The Shyness and Social Anxiety Workbook: Proven, Step-by-Step Techniques for Overcoming Your Fear*. 2nd ed. Oakland, CA: New Harbinger Publications.

Bögels, S. M., G. F. V. M. Sijbers, and M. Voncken. 2006. "Mindfulness and Task Concentration Training for Social Phobia: A Pilot Study." *Journal of Cognitive Psychotherapy* 20 (1):33–44.

Chabris, C. F., and D. J. Simons. 2010. *The Invisible Gorilla: How Our Intuitions Deceive Us*. New York: Crown Publishers.

Cullen, M. 2011. "Mindfulness-Based Interventions: An Emerging Phenomenon." *Mindfulness* 2 (3):186–93.

Dalrymple, K. L., and J. D. Herbert. 2007. "Acceptance and Commitment Therapy for Generalized Social Anxiety Disorder: A Pilot Study." *Behavior Modification* 31 (5):543–68.

Ellis, A. 1994. *Reason and Emotion in Psychotherapy: A Comprehensive Method of Treating Human Disturbances. Revised and Updated*. New York: Citadel Press.

Gilovich, T., and K. Savitsky. 1999. "The Spotlight Effect and the Illusion of Transparency: Egocentric Assessments of How We Are Seen by Others." *Current Directions in Psychological Science* 8 (6):165–68.

Goldin, P., W. Ramel, and J. Gross. 2009. "Mindfulness Meditation Training and Self-Referential Processing in Social Anxiety Disorder: Behavioral and Neural Effects." *Journal of Cognitive Psychotherapy* 23 (3):242–57.

Hampson, S. 2012. "Should We Trust Our Inner Cheerleaders? New Research Says We Should Pay Attention to Our 'Self-Talk' and Learn to Evaluate It Realistically." *The Globe and Mail*, February 27.

Harris, R. 2008. *The Happiness Trap: How to Stop Struggling and Start Living.* Boston: Trumpeter Books.

———. 2009. *ACT Made Simple: An Easy-to-Read Primer on Acceptance and Commitment Therapy.* Oakland, CA: New Harbinger Publications.

Hayes, S. C. 2005. *Get Out of Your Mind and Into Your Life: The New Acceptance and Commitment Therapy.* With S. Smith. Oakland, CA: New Harbinger Publications.

Hayes, S. C., K. D. Strosahl, and K. G. Wilson. 1999. *Acceptance and Commitment Therapy: An Experiential Approach to Behavior Change.* New York: The Guilford Press.

Heimberg, R. G. 2002. "Cognitive-Behavioral Therapy for Social Anxiety Disorder: Current Status and Future Directions." *Biological Psychiatry* 51 (1):101–108.

Kabat-Zinn, J. 1990. *Full Catastrophe Living: Using the Wisdom of Your Body and Mind to Face Stress, Pain, and Illness.* New York: Dell Publishing.

———. 1994. *Wherever You Go, There You Are: Mindfulness Meditation in Everyday Life.* New York: Hyperion.

Kocovski, N.L., J.E. Fleming, L.L. Hawley, V. Huta, and M.M. Antony. Under review. "Mindfulness and Acceptance-Based Group Therapy versus Traditional Cognitive Behavioral Group Therapy for Social Anxiety Disorder: A Randomized Controlled Trial."

Kocovski, N. L., J. E. Fleming, and N. A. Rector. 2009. "Mindfulness and Acceptance-Based Group Therapy for Social Anxiety Disorder: An Open Trial." *Cognitive and Behavioral Practice* 16 (3):276–89.

Koszycki, D., M. Benger, J. Shlik, and J. Bradwejn. 2007. "Randomized Trial of a Meditation-Based Stress Reduction Program and Cognitive Behavior Therapy in Generalized Social Anxiety Disorder." *Behaviour Research and Therapy* 45 (10):2518–26.

Morén, K., and C. Wiwe. 2006. "Comparing Acceptance and Commitment Therapy and Cognitive Behavioural Therapy for Social Anxiety Disorder: A Randomized Controlled Trial." Presentation at The Second World Conference on ACT, RFT, and Contextual Behavioural Science, July 27, London.

Neff, K. D. 2012. "The Science of Self-Compassion." In *Wisdom and Compassion in Psychotherapy: Deepening Mindfulness in Clinical Practice*, edited by C. K. Germer and R. D. Siegel, 79–92. New York: The Guilford Press.

Ossman, W. A., K. G. Wilson, R. D. Storaasli, and J. W. McNeill. 2006. "A Preliminary Investigation of the Use of Acceptance and Commitment Therapy in Group Treatment for Social Phobia." *International Journal of Psychology and Psychological Therapy* 6 (3):397–416.

Piet, J., and E. Hougaard. 2011. "The Effect of Mindfulness-Based Cognitive Therapy for Prevention of Relapse in Recurrent Major Depressive Disorder: A Systematic Review and Meta-Analysis." *Clinical Psychology Review* 31 (6):1032–40.

Piet, J., E. Hougaard, M. S. Hecksher, and N. K. Rosenberg. 2010. "A Randomized Pilot Study of Mindfulness-Based Cognitive Therapy and Group Cognitive-Behavioral Therapy for Young Adults with Social Phobia." *Scandinavian Journal of Psychology* 51:403–10.

Ruiz, F. J. 2010. "A Review of Acceptance and Commitment Therapy (ACT) Empirical Evidence: Correlational, Experimental Psychopathology, Component and Outcome Studies." *International Journal of Psychology and Psychological Therapy* 10 (1):125–62.

Ruscio, A. M., T. A. Brown, W. T. Chiu, J. Sareen, M. B. Stein, and R. C. Kessler. 2008. "Social Fears and Social Phobia in the USA: Results from the National Comorbidity Survey Replication." *Psychological Medicine* 38 (1):15–28.

Segal, Z. V., J. M. G. Williams, and J. D. Teasdale. 2002. *Mindfulness-Based Cognitive Therapy for Depression: A New Approach to Preventing Relapse.* New York: The Guilford Press.

Silverstein, S. 2009. "Fear." In *A Light in the Attic*, special ed. New York: HarperCollins.

Sloan Wilson, D., A. B. Clark, K. Coleman, and T. Dearstyne. 1994. "Shyness and Boldness in Humans and Other Animals." *Trends in Ecology and Evolution* 9 (11):442–46.

Wilson, K. G., and T. Dufrene. 2010. *Things Might Go Terribly, Horribly Wrong: A Guide to Life Liberated from Anxiety*. Oakland, CA: New Harbinger Publications.

Jan E. Fleming, MD, is associate clinical professor of psychiatry at the University of Toronto, ON, Canada, staff psychiatrist in the Anxiety Disorders Clinic at the Centre for Addiction and Mental Health, and clinical associate at The Mindfulness Clinic, all located in Toronto, ON. She has been a fellow of the Royal College of Physicians and Surgeons of Canada and a practicing psychiatrist for over twenty-five years. As a founding member of the Offord Centre for Child Studies in Hamilton, ON, she received support from the Ontario Mental Health Foundation, the Ontario Ministry of Health, and the National Alliance for Research on Schizophrenia and Depression, for her research on adolescent depression. Currently, her research and clinical focus are on the application of mindfulness and acceptance-based approaches—such as acceptance and commitment therapy—to social anxiety disorder.

Nancy L. Kocovski, PhD, is associate professor of psychology at Wilfrid Laurier University in Waterloo, ON, Canada, where she teaches in the area of clinical psychology and maintains an active research program focused on social anxiety, mindfulness and acceptance-based treatments, and cognitive behavior therapy (CBT). She received a New Investigator Fellowship from the Ontario Mental Health Foundation for her work on the development of mindfulness and acceptance-based group therapy for social anxiety disorder. She received an Early Researcher Award from the Ministry of Research and Innovation in Ontario for her work on social anxiety and mindfulness. Kocovski also works as a clinical psychologist in private practice at CBT Associates of Toronto.

Fleming and Kocovski have worked closely together for almost a decade to develop and test the mindfulness and acceptance-based approach outlined in this book. Their research has shown the approach to be as effective as traditional cognitive behavior therapy in alleviating the suffering associated with social anxiety disorder.

Foreword writer **Zindel V. Segal, PhD**, is professor of psychology at the University of Toronto-Scarborough, Toronto, ON, Canada. He is author of *Mindfulness-Based Cognitive Therapy for Depression* and *The Mindful Way through Depression*.

For more information visit www.actonsocialanxiety.com.

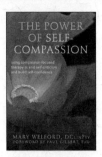

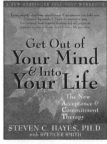

FROM OUR PUBLISHER—

As the publisher at New Harbinger and a clinical psychologist since 1978, I know that emotional problems are best helped with evidence-based therapies. These are the treatments derived from scientific research (randomized controlled trials) that show what works. Whether these treatments are delivered by trained clinicians or found in a self-help book, they are designed to provide you with proven strategies to overcome your problem.

Therapies that aren't evidence-based—whether offered by clinicians or in books—are much less likely to help. In fact, therapies that aren't guided by science may not help you at all. That's why this New Harbinger book is based on scientific evidence that the treatment can relieve emotional pain.

This is important: if this book isn't enough, and you need the help of a skilled therapist, use the following resources to find a clinician trained in the evidence-based protocols appropriate for your problem. And if you need more support—a community that understands what you're going through and can show you ways to cope—resources for that are provided below, as well.

Real help is available for the problems you have been struggling with. The skills you can learn from evidence-based therapies will change your life.

Matthew McKay, PhD
Publisher, New Harbinger Publications

new harbinger
CELEBRATING
40 YEARS

**If you need a therapist, the following organization can help you
find a therapist trained in acceptance and commitment therapy (ACT).**

Association for Contextual Behavioral Science (ACBS)
please visit www.contextualscience.org and click on *Find an ACT Therapist*.

**For additional support for patients, family, and friends,
please contact the following:**

Anxiety and Depression Association of American (ADAA)
please visit www.adaa.org

National Alliance on Mental Illness (NAMI)
please visit www.nami.org

Register your **new harbinger** titles for additional benefits!

When you register your **new harbinger** title—purchased in any format, from any source—you get access to benefits like the following:

- Downloadable accessories like printable worksheets and extra content
- Instructional videos and audio files
- Information about updates, corrections, and new editions

Not every title has accessories, but we're adding new material all the time.

Access free accessories in 3 easy steps:

1. Sign in at NewHarbinger.com (or **register** to create an account).

2. Click on **register a book**. Search for your title and click the **register** button when it appears.

3. Click on the **book cover or title** to go to its details page. Click on **accessories** to view and access files.

That's all there is to it!

If you need help, visit:

NewHarbinger.com/accessories

new harbinger
CELEBRATING
40 YEARS